Exploring the Northern Tradition

A Guide to the Gods, Lore, Rites, and Celebrations From the Norse, German, and Anglo-Saxon Traditions

By

Galina Krasskova

Foreword by Swain Wodening, cofounder of the Angelseaxisce Ealdriht

New Page Books
A division of The Career Press, Inc.
Franklin Lakes, NJ

EXPLORING THE NORTHERN TRADITION
EDITED BY CLAYTON W. LEADBETTER
TYPESET BY EILEEN DOW MUNSON
Cover illustration and design by Jean William Naumann
Printed in the U.S.A. by Courier

To order this title, please call toll-free 1-800-CAREER-1 (NJ and Canada: 201-848-0310) to order using VISA or MasterCard, or for further information on books from Career Press.

The Career Press, Inc., 3 Tice Road, PO Box 687,
Franklin Lakes, NJ 07417
www.careerpress.com
www.newpagebooks.com

Library of Congress Cataloging-in-Publication Data

Krasskova, Galina, 1972-
Exploring the northern tradition : a guide to the gods, lore, rites, and celebrations from the Norse, German, and Anglo-Saxon traditions / by Galina Krasskova ; foreword by Swain Wodening.
p. cm.
Includes bibliographical references (p.) and index.
ISBN 1-56414-791-6 (paper)
1. Germanic peoples—Religion. 2. Mythology, Germanic. I. Title.

BL860.K73 2005
293—dc22

2004060870

This book is lovingly dedicated

to my great, great, great grandmother,

Elizabeth Oberlander Runkle,

in gratitude for her care and assistance.

Acknowledgments

Like any creative work, this book has been, in many ways, a collaborative effort. It could not have been written save for the unwavering support and inspiration of a number of people, both within the Heathen community and without. So many folks offered their support in the most unexpected of ways that they deserve recognition here.

First and foremost, I would like to thank three people who have nourished me spiritually and supported me in ways that leave me awed and grateful: K.C. Hulsman, Fuensanta Plaza, and Jason Barnes. You've been pillars of sanity in a mad, chaotic, and frustrating world. I don't think I would even have had the wherewithal to begin this project but for your encouragement and support. Thank you.

I would like to thank the good folk of Neoweanglia Maethel and her lord Brian Hlaford Smith for their encouragement. I'd especially like to thank Wulfgaest, Heah Blotere of the Haligwaerstow, for his continued support and translation assistance.

A special thank you to Lord Dan O'Halloran, Aetheling Lord of Normanni Reiks, for permission to use his quote on the subject of Symbel.

I am deeply indebted to Rev. Sharon Breland, for her keen eye in proofreading, and to K.C. Hulsman, for allowing me the use of her master's thesis as a resource.

I would also like to acknowledge, with deepest gratitude, the Ealdriht's Swain Aetheling Wodening and his lady Tee Hlafdige Wodening.

I am also grateful to Krei Steinberg, gythia of Whirling Wheel Kindred; Raven Kaldera and all the "grouchy spiritworkers," for being a much-needed sanity valve; Ruther Skae; Aleksa Pacuska; Dave Ryan; Hanshi Rico Guy and Kyoshi Penny Johnson; Ramodolc Ennovy Enicnarf; Rev. Francesca Fortunato; Rev. Hal Shaw; MM (just because); Christine Kulawas, Esq.; the entire team of the DB Microcredit and Community Development Department (for tolerating my varying degrees of insanity as my deadline drew near and for being the first to celebrate my pending book); and last, but not by any means least, the editorial staff of New Page Books. You have been a true pleasure to work with and this book could never have taken form were it not for your support. Any errors contained within this text are entirely my own.

Contents

Foreword

Heathen—the word is used to conjure up images of savages without deities, roughing it in the wild...impolite, with no manners and very low technology. Yet the word *Heathen* once referred to a fairly technologically advanced people with a very complex religion not unlike modern Hinduism. Today, *Heathenry* denotes the modern revival of the ancient Germanic religions, once known as *Asatru* (although Asatru now only refers to the Icelandic version of Germanic Heathenry). The revival of the ancient Germanic religions (there were many different tribal variations and are many different denominations today) began more than 30 years ago, nearly simultaneously, in the Americas, Iceland, and Great Britain. At first, these distant groups of worshippers did not know of each other, but in time, they did learn of one another. Since then the number of practitioners of Heathenry has continued to grow, both in individual worshippers and in the different denominations that follow it. There are now Heathens following Norse, Anglo-Saxon, Gothic, and other Germanic paths, as well as several national and international organizations devoted to the furtherance of the religions as a whole.

All of this happened despite the fact that very few books have been written on the modern practice of Heathenry and that what few have been published have been in print for very short periods of time. Galina Krasskova has, therefore, produced something very needed and longed for: a book introducing folks new to Heathenry to the religion. She covers all the basics, such as the evolution of modern Heathenry, its ethics, the concept of Wyrd, rites, and other things necessary for someone new to the religion to know. Her documentation is extensive, and those wishing to learn should by all means read the works she references, as well as those she lists in the bibliography. Heathenry is very much a religion with homework, and values the quest for wisdom as much as it does the quest for spirituality.

—Swain Wodening
Author of *Hammer of the Gods: Anglo-Saxon Paganism in Modern Times*

Introduction

To most people, the word *heathen* is a pejorative, usually taken to indicate a godless or uncivilized person. If the listener is particularly enlightened, it may instead be understood to refer to one who does not worship the Abrahamic God, which is at least partially accurate. What most folks fail to realize is that, today, *Heathen* has also come to designate a unique and sacred identity for those who have returned to the worship of the pre-Christian Gods of Northern Europe. In fact, there is a growing religious movement, not only in America but across the world, of people who have chosen to honor the Gods and Goddesses of the pre-Christian Scandinavian, Germanic, and English world. They belong to a number of denominations in the modern rebirth of an ancient faith and call themselves Heathens. In the following chapters, we will examine why. Thousands and thousands of people are reconstructing the ancient rites, praying to the ancient Gods—Odin, Thor, Frigga, Freya, and Their kin—and remembering and honoring their ancestors in ways that reflect the wisdom and knowledge of this sacred tradition.

I became Heathen in 1996. By that time, I had been a priestess in the Fellowship of Isis (an eclectic Pagan organization dedicated to the promulgation and exploration of Goddess Spirituality[1]) for a number of years. I was an experienced ritual worker with a well-defined personal theology of practice. I never, ever, expected to end up Heathen. In the nine years that I have been Heathen, I have seen my religious community grow and evolve, developing a strong cultural identity. I have watched as our spiritual focus deepened and as we began to examine our faith not only as religion but also as a folkway—a set of cultural and ethical parameters by which we were committed to living as we practiced our faith. One thing I have not seen, however, was an effective means by which to welcome newcomers into the tradition. Not only did I never expect to find myself drawn to Heathenry at all, in fact, I had a rather negative impression of the religion precisely because of the lack of friendly welcome to newcomers. At the same time, there were many things about the religion that attracted me. First and foremost, I became Heathen because I fell in love with the God Woden. Certainly, I appreciated the strong warrior ethic found in Heathenry, but for the most part, I was seduced by Woden. If not for that attachment and devotion, it would have taken me far longer to accept the identity of Heathen for myself. This puts me in an unusual category amongst Heathens, because the impetus that drew me to Heathenry was not lore, culture, or ethics. I came to Heathenry because of personal experience with a particular God, and I came to Heathenry with several years as a priest and pastoral counselor under my proverbial belt. Those experiences have continued to define my beliefs and practice.

There are two terms that anyone interested in Heathenry should be familiar with: *lore* and *UPG*. Anyone with even passing familiarity with Asatru and Heathenry will hear the word *lore* used by practitioners—often accompanied by quotes from obscure Icelandic or Germanic texts. For the modern Heathen, much of the practical application of our sacred tradition is drawn from clues found in the Icelandic Sagas; the Poetic and Prose Eddas; Anglo-Saxon historical, legal, and medical texts; as well as modern archaeological, linguistic, and anthropological research. Studying these texts is very nearly a devotional experience for most Heathens, and this body of work is generally referred to as "the Lore." Heathens explore and debate these texts in much the same way as a traditional Talmudic scholar might explore and debate the commentary on the Torah. In some cases, unfortunately, such debate has taken the place of personal devotion. In others, it naturally augments and supports such devotion. But for anyone coming into Heathenry, a basic knowledge of *at least* the Eddas and Icelandic Sagas is de rigueur. Such knowledge will go a long way toward ensuring a warm welcome from the community at large. Because we, as Heathens, are seeking to restore a spiritual and cultural tradition that was largely destroyed by the arrival and spread of Christianity across Europe, we draw upon clues found in the lore to ensure that our practices are as logically consistent with the practices of our ancestors as possible. While changes and additions are being made, given that we live in a drastically different time and place, they are done so within a coherent historical and lore-based framework. This ensures that our modern religion remains attuned to the spirit of the original practice. While we don't know exactly how pre-Christian Heathens practiced, we can draw reasonable conclusions from the surviving manuscripts.

The second term one should be familiar with is *UPG*. UPG stands for "Unverified Personal Gnosis." Within the Heathen community, this term is used for those experiences and spiritual epiphanies that, while very powerful on an individual level, are completely unverifiable by surviving Heathen lore. Acceptance of UPGs varies from community to community, with some granting far more credence to direct experience than others. It is one of the major divisions within Heathenry today: what should hold greater prominence—mystical experience or metaphysical orthodoxy? As a priest, I've long believed that the two should walk hand in hand. Mysticism (that is, personal experience) is limited, if not useless, without the ability to communicate it effectively. Lore provides the framework in which those direct experiences can be processed, understood, and communicated. At the same time, there comes a point at which the authority of lore must bow its head to the realities of experience or risk becoming a brittle parody of spirituality.

There are times when a given UPG is so commonly found across all segments of the community that it becomes accepted as modern lore. For instance, it is commonly accepted in modern Heathenry that the *valknot*, a sacred symbol comprised of three interlocking triangles, is sacred to the God Odin (or Woden, to give Him His Anglo-Saxon name[2]). Nowhere in the surviving lore is this stated. The valknot, however, is found carved on several runestones, in every case in association with sacrifice, warriors, and the valkyries—all things strongly associated with Odin in the lore. Modern Heathens, through personal experience with this God, have taken this to its reasonably logical conclusion and given

Him the symbol. It would take a bold Heathen indeed to wear a valknot when he or she was NOT dedicated to Odin.[3] Another commonly accepted UPG is that the Goddess Freya likes offerings of strawberries. It's not written anywhere in the lore, but so many people have had this particular UPG in the Heathen community that it has gained overall acceptance.

Understanding the difference between these two terms and being able to accurately clarify when an experience is UPG and when it is soundly grounded in lore is a necessity within Heathenry. By and large, the Heathen community is fairly conservative. Change is accepted slowly and only after much consideration. In our efforts to maintain our cultural and religious integrity, UPG is occasionally greeted with skepticism. There is a deep aversion to Neo-Paganism and particularly to Eclectic Wicca amongst most Heathens. Heathenry is not a Neo-Pagan faith, nor does it bear any connection to Wicca. We do, however, have a large percentage of converts coming from Wicca and generic Neo-Paganism, and there is something of a backlash within the community against any lingering Neo-Pagan influence. As an indigenous tradition, most modern Heathens guard the integrity of their religious culture assiduously. This creates some problems for the newcomer, which I hope to address in this book.

It's important to remember that few of us were raised honoring the Gods and Goddesses. It's fairly safe to say that most of us were raised in one of the dominant religions of our culture: Christianity, Judaism, or possibly Islam. For many raised in the more fundamentalist denominations of these religions, coming to an awareness of and devotion to the Heathen Gods can be a terrifying experience, often fraught with guilt. Converting to any religion has its difficulties. Converting to the worship of Gods one has traditionally been taught to think of as nonexistent, archetypal, or in many cases, evil can be all the more difficult.

There are few resources in the Heathen community to smooth such a transition. If the convert is very lucky, he or she will find a competent Heathen clergyperson who remembers the difficulties of her own early days in the religion. But often, that is simply not the case—there is no one available, there is no Heathen community where the new convert lives, or the only clergy available in the local Heathen community are unfamiliar with the conversion process or untrained in the subtleties of pastoral counseling.[4] E-mail lists are harsh and often unfriendly to the newcomer who may know little of lore or Heathen social structure. The only books out there are either out-of-date or geared toward the New Age community rather than the Heathen. Often there is no family support during this time. It can be a frustrating experience.

One helpful thing to remember is that our spirituality did not evolve in a vacuum; it's not a matter of suddenly excising the lessons with which we were brought up, but of evolving and adding yet another layer to the tapestry of our sacred landscape. For instance, I was raised Catholic and, though I left the church when quite young, I still draw immense spiritual nourishment from the writings of the Rhine mystics, from C.S. Lewis, and from renegade modern mystic Matthew Fox.[5] It was from my Catholic grandmother that I first learned to value the spiritual, and from the writings of the Rhine mystics, long-dead women of a religion I no longer practice, that I learned the importance of prayer and, more importantly, how to pray. It's not an either/or scenario, and none of us go to the Gods as blank religious slates.

Therefore, for one newly emerging into the Heathen faith, it's important to realize that it's okay to cull the beautiful devotional aspects of one's own faith. There's nothing wrong with that. It provides a bridge to the new, and this is a good thing. While purists may rage against anything smacking of syncretization, it is often a necessary and usually temporary step in one's spiritual journey.[6] Understand this and, if necessary, allow yourself the necessary transitional time. Moreover, there are commonalities to the spiritual experience that transcend the barriers of denomination and religion. Great comfort and understanding can be achieved by the reading of shared experience—even if that experience occurs across religious lines. Find what nourishes you in your religion of birth. Find those things that help you move forward toward greater awareness of the Gods. These are good and essential building blocks of faith.

This is actually something of a heretical idea in most Heathen circles, but the realities of conversion vary greatly from person to person; it is a simple fact that some may need the added comfort of that transitional time. Do I advocate dual-tradition allegiance? No, not really. But I understand the necessities of the human heart. The way in which we begin to allow ourselves to see the Gods is determined largely by the religion in which we were raised. Rather than fighting against that, it is far more effective to use it to one's advantage. Throughout the course of this book, I will provide suggestions and exercises that will aid the newcomer to Heathenry not only in learning about our Gods and learning about lore, but in developing a strong personal discipline of devotion. Being Heathen is more than simply honoring the Norse Gods, but that is certainly a good place to begin.

In the following chapters, I will take you through everything you need to know to confidently enter into the Heathen community—from the history of Heathenry and its modern rebirth to our fundamental theological tenets. We will examine the ethics and values of modern Heathenry, the nature of our Gods and Goddesses, the fundamentals of Heathen rituals, and the building blocks of personal devotion. It is my sincere hope that this simple volume provides a thorough introduction to Heathenry, not only for the new convert but for anyone interested in learning about the modern resurgence of an ancient, indigenous faith.

April 16, 2004
New York City

Chapter 1

The Evolution of Modern Heathenry

There was a time when Northern Europe was completely Heathen. Of course, the term *Heathenry* wasn't used; that came later, with the insurgence of Christianity and the need to give a derogatory name to the old religious beliefs that were not so easily discarded by the people. There was no specific name for the common faith practiced by the Germanic, Scandinavian, and English tribes, and none was needed. It was simply what they believed, what their ancestors before them had believed, and what had kept their communities strong and whole for generations. Fragments of their practices have come down to us in the Eddas, Sagas, histories, medical charms, and even Christian ecclesiastical writings. Theirs was not a single religion as modern theology might define it, but a collection of tribal religions with a common, cohesive, cosmological core. They shared a belief in the same Gods, though many regional variations on the divine names were known. They shared a common system of honoring those Gods, common ethics and values, and widespread veneration of their honored dead. At various times and in various regions, different Gods may have held local prominence, but the core beliefs were similar.

As early as 98 C.E., the Roman historian Tacitus recorded the religious practices of the British Isles, noting that "their holy places are woods and groves, and they apply the names of Deities to that hidden presence which is seen only by the eye of reverence."[1] He examined, at length, the various governments of the Germanic tribes, their social customs, and the high regard in which they held their women. His is the only surviving record of the Goddess Nerthus, whose worship was once widespread throughout the North. Another important source of information was the eyewitness accounts of Arab travelers Ibn Fadlan and at-Tartusi. Given that the Germanic and Scandinavian tribes were primarily oral in nature, we are forced to rely on these firsthand accounts of travelers, tradesman, and diplomats and on the writings of Christian historians and scribes for the majority of surviving material on religious customs and beliefs. The primary source of information comes from the Viking Age, 800 C.E. to 1300 C.E. This was a time of extensive interaction both through trade, migration, and violent raiding. Viking trade routes spanned the continent of Europe, extending throughout the North, to what is now modern-day Russia and even as far as the Ottoman Empire.[2] At least 100 years after the fall of the last Heathen temple in 1100 C.E., we have the Icelandic statesman and poet, Snorri Sturluson, committing to print the tales and sagas of the Gods and mighty heroes.

Given the extensive trade routes maintained by the Vikings, the inevitable intermarriage with other cultures, the prevalence of Saami references in the context of Nordic magico-religious practices, and the occasional reference in lore to folk who worshipped both Thor and Christ, it's doubtful that there was any strict rigid Heathen orthodoxy. The ease with which early Christian healers combined Heathen and Christian symbology in their healing charms would also support this fact. According to Thomas Dubois, the scholarship of recent decades confirms a far more culturally interconnected worldview of Viking Age Europe between the Anglo-Saxons, Balto-Finnic, Celtic, Saami, and Norse cultures.[3] Furthermore, there would have been no need for such orthodoxy; the religion was not in opposition to the dominant culture. As with many polytheistic cultures, the initial attitude toward foreign Gods was quite likely not hostile. The difference is that any religion they came in contact with prior to the advent of Christianity would have been grounded in the specific cultures of its adherents, providing a logical continuity of cosmological understanding. Such religions would only become a threat once their dogmatic imperative became the dissolution and destruction of other beliefs.

Unfortunately, this is precisely what occurred with Christianity. The arrival of Christianity in Northern Europe was inevitably followed by prohibitions curtailing the practice of the indigenous faiths.[4] Some of the more zealous converted Christian Kings, such as Norway's King Olaf Tryggvason,[5] enforced those prohibitions with violent, blood-thirsty zeal, torturing followers of the old Gods with a viciousness matched only by the later Spanish Inquisition. Christianity appeared in England with the arrival of Augustine, sent at Pope Gregory's behest in 597 C.E. In less than 200 years, England was thoroughly Christianized, though Heathen practices and customs apparently continued to coexist alongside the newfound faith. According to Swain Wodening, "Heathen Gods were still being invoked in charms for healing as late as the 10th century. As late as the reign of King Canute in the 11th century, laws had to be enacted against Heathen practices."[6]

The rest of Northern Europe fell to Christian ideological conquest slowly but surely. Iceland converted in 1000 C.E.,[7] when their lawspeaker, Thorgeirr Thorkelsson, was asked to mediate the growing dispute between Christian and Heathen factions. He withdrew "under the cloak"[8] for a day and a night and, when he emerged, settled in favor of the Christians. The last Heathen Temple, in Uppsala, Sweden, was forcibly closed in 1100 C.E. after the defeat of King Sweyn "the Sacrificer." King Sweyn had taken the throne after his brother in law, King Inge I was ousted for trying to impose Christianity upon the people. Inge later raised an army, killed Sweyn, and took back his throne, and Christianity became the state religion. This slow process of conversion was not without its attendant bloodshed on both sides as this latter example illustrates.

The conversion of Europe was finalized by historians and scholars who inevitably reinforced the idea of Christianity as a positive evolution of belief, regardless of the cultural and religious devastation it left in its wake (insofar as the indigenous practices were concerned). Little attention has been given to pre-Christian Heathenry as a serious faith, and modern scholars remain equally dismissive of the rebirth of Heathenry, expressing biased, condescending, or antiquated views.[9] Given the growing number of folk embracing modern Heathenry and its growth as a religion, the resistance of modern theologians and scholars toward comparative examination of this faith remains a mystery.

Through the relentless spread of Christianity across Northern Europe, Heathen practice officially came to an end in 1100 C.E. Slowly, the tribal laws and ethics began to give way to Christian ones. Though folk traditions remained alive and well in Scandinavian, English, and Germanic countries, the Nordic Gods were not openly worshipped again on any large scale until the 1970s. Some modern Heathens refer to those Heathens of pre-Christian Europe as "Arch-Heathens." Because they lived in a time when their faith and culture was able to develop not only without interference but without being in conflict with the dominant cultural and social mores, it is thought that they had a clearer connection to the Gods—something that only this generation's children's children, raised Heathen, will have a chance to reclaim.

The rebirth of modern Heathenry actually began in late-19th-century Germany. German Romanticism saw a burgeoning interest in the tales and fables of the old Gods. The occult revival of the West, so well represented by Dion Fortune, Helena Blavatsky, and yes, even Aleister Crowley, had its German counterparts in Guido von List, Rudolf Steiner, and the Thule Society. Just as the occult revival in England led eventually to the birth of Modern Wicca, so Heathenry may have also gone a similar route had World War II not interfered. Modern Heathens are often asked if their religion has anything to do with Nazism or racism. The answer is an unequivocal no. It is true that Nazi Germany took certain sacred Heathen symbols, such as the sun wheel (a symbol of the regenerative power of the sun found in nearly every Indo-European culture and even in Japan) and various runes. However, they were not Heathen, nor did Hitler and his Nazis ascribe to any Heathen practices or beliefs. In fact, Hitler several times expressed very negative views about followers of the old Gods, and in 1941, the head of his security police, Reinhardt Heydrich, banned a large number of spiritual and occult practices. Among the victims of this act were followers of Rudolf Steiner, Guido von List, and traditional Odinists (worshippers of the God Odin). Many were arrested. Their property was confiscated, and some were even sent to concentration camps such as Flossenberg and Dachau.[10] Of course there will always be ignorant folk who attempt to misuse our sacred symbols. Unfortunately there is a small percentage of racists who attempt to latch on to Heathen principles in an effort to further their hate-filled agenda. However, the majority of modern Heathens find them deplorable and will have nothing to do with them.

World War II set the rebirth of Modern Heathenry back at least 30 years. It wasn't until the early 1970s that it truly began to grow again. Groups in Iceland, America, and England and across Europe, independently of each other, began to worship the Norse Gods and reconstruct Heathen rituals and practices. Icelandic poet and farmer Sveinbjorn Beinteinsson formed the group Asatruarfelagid with his friends. Robert Stine and Stephen McNallon, in the United Sates, formed the Viking Brotherhood, which was later renamed the Asatru Folk Alliance. The Committee for the Restoration of the Odinic Rite was formed in the United Kingdom by John Yeowell and his associates.[11] The decades that followed saw immense growth in the Heathen community and also schisms and splits, as opinions on formation and practice diverged. New groups, such as Thaet Angelseaxisce Ealdriht, devoted to the study and practice of Anglo-Saxon forms of Heathenry; Normanni Thiud, focusing on Norman Heathenry; and The Troth, an international networking organization, soon sprang up across the United States. In 1973, Asatru[12] was named one of the official religions of Iceland. It took equal place alongside the Lutheran Church. In 2003, the Lutheran Church in Denmark (which possesses ultimate religious authority in that country) granted official status to a Heathen religious group, which can now perform legal Heathen weddings.

Like any other religion, modern Heathenry is quite diverse and it has many different denominations. I will briefly touch on the best known. It's important to remember that, while all modern Heathens share a common cosmological core, social structure and theological emphasis and approach can vary widely from group to group. At its broadest base, modern Heathenry can best be divided by where the groups draw their primary cultural impetus. The major denominations pull upon Icelandic, Continental Germanic and Scandinavian, Anglo-Saxon, or Norman history, culture, language, and religion for their reconstructionist inspiration. Some focus on one particular culture, while others may draw from several or even all of the above.

The three terms that newcomers to the community will invariably hear are (1) Tribalist, (2) Universalist, and (3) Folkish.

These aren't really denominations so much as a socio-political-religious spectrum into which various denominations of Heathenry may fall. Within that spectrum, there are strict reconstructionists who restrict their practices to what can clearly and unarguably be referenced from the surviving lore. There are neo-Heathens who are far more innovative and open to exploring resources that are not lore-based (such a Harner's Core Shamanism) and who focus on the modern evolution of Heathenry (what would Heathenry be like had we not endured 2,000 years of Christianity?). There are also those Heathens who fall somewhere between the two, as well as those who believe that Heathenry, like Shinto and like the Native American religions, is an indigenous religion and should be approached as such. Some Heathens may even fall into more than one category. For instance, one may be Tribalist but believe that Heathenry is also an indigenous tradition. Let's examine each, in turn, beginning with the one that falls in the middle of the spectrum.

- **Tribalism:** Some groups, such as Thaet Angelseaxisce Ealdriht and Normanni Thiud, are Tribalist—focused on rebuilding cohesive, interdependent communities structured around strict adherence to the Heathen thew of our ancestors. These denominations tend to have hierarchical social structures based on the comitatus model of the Anglo-Saxons and Normans and tend to be somewhat conservative. They are not inclusive generally, expecting a certain degree of commitment and demonstrated worth from new members. Among Tribalist Heathens, the family and community are the binding forces by which the individual Heathens govern their lives. Much focus is paid to right action and right relationship, the accepted definition of frith being far more active and assertive than other denominations may expect. As with other denominations of Heathenry, honoring the Gods, blóting, and celebrating the holy tides are all considered extremely important. Religion, community, and culture are inseparable, being seen as necessary components to a well-balanced whole. The Tribal community is generally the primary means of self-definition for Tribalist Heathens.

- **Universalism:** At the more liberal end of the spectrum, we have Universalist Heathens (a good example would be the majority of the Troth community). They generally tend to be far more tolerant of variations of thew and practice. There is less concern for social organization or a centralized authority, and they reject the hierarchical, theodish social structure and the need for a web of oaths (which we will discuss below). They generally appreciate diversity, and socially, there is no focus on building insular Heathen communities, as their self-definition does not rest on the tribal unit but rather on the individual. There is far more focus amongst Universalists on getting along with other Heathens and accommodating variances in practice than will be found amongst Tribalists. Comparatively, they are understanding, if not accepting, of Neo-Pagan influence; many Universalists even consider Heathenry to fall under the Neo-Pagan umbrella—a position most Folkish Heathens and Tribalists reject. There is more focus on the commonality of cosmological symbolism between cultures and religions (a la Joseph Campbell) and far more focus on commonalties between Heathens rather than on cultural uniqueness. As with Tribalists, honoring the Gods, studying lore, and keeping the holy tides are all very important parts of Universalist practice.
- **Folkish Heathenry:** At the more conservative end of the spectrum, we have Folkish Heathenry. Perhaps no other "denomination" causes such controversy as this one does. When I first became Heathen in 1996, "Folkish" was used interchangeably with "racist," denoting a person one step away from being a White Supremacist. Thankfully, over the years, this reactionary view has softened somewhat and we are now seeing a spectrum of belief and practice within the Folkish community. At the base level, Folkish Heathens believe that, in order to practice Heathenry, one must be either of English/Germanic/Scandinavian descent or acculturated to such a community. For some, those who are not of European descent may become part of the community by adoption or blood-sib oath. For others, nothing less than English/Germanic/Scandinavian blood ancestry will suffice. Like Tribalists, there is a strong focus on building a strong Heathen community (and many Folkish Heathens are also Tribalist). Heathenry, however, is seen as an ancestral religion first and foremost; to appreciate it fully—to

truly have a direct link to the Norse Gods—one must share in that ancestry. Most Folkish Heathens would not consider themselves racist (though there is that percentage of the community as well) but would simply not comprehend why someone of non-Germanic descent would choose to honor Germanic Gods and culture. Such a person would be encouraged to seek out and honor his or her own indigenous Gods. The Asatru Alliance is one example of a Folkish Organization. This is where it becomes tricky: While some small percentage of Folkish Heathens may be racist, it does not follow that Folkism is automatically synonymous with racism. In most cases, it is not. The defining tenet of Folkish Heathenry is that Heathenry is seen, first and foremost, as an ancestral tradition.

- **Theodish Heathenry:** There is another term that folks should be familiar with: Theodish Heathenry. The most defining factor about Theodish Heathens is that, within the tribal structure, they are bound by what is called a "web of oaths." Tribal bonds are formed between individuals of varying social rank (and Theodish social structure is hierarchical), by means of sacred oath. It is this web of oaths that holds the entire tribe together. To quote one of the founding mothers of Winland Rice, Gert McQueen, on the nature of tribal social structure:

> "The structure covers three types of areas: social, religious, and crafts. Each of these areas functions with a system of ranks and oaths of loyalty. It is possible for an individual to have rank in all three areas in varying degrees. Or an individual could be content to be of the lowest rank and still be bound by the oaths that bind him together within the structure. These ranks reflect not only the degree to which an individual has proven his devotion, knowledge and wisdom, but also the degree of responsibility that that individual carries. Rank means responsibility for and to others. Theodish Heathenry has traditions, values, ethics, and rules of conduct and proper behavior that are enforced through customary law and pertain to every level of Heathen society. If an individual does not or cannot conduct himself according to customary law he is then removed from the society, for he is a threat to the well-being of the whole.

> The web of oaths is not in a democratic spirit. There are no equal rights across the board in Theodish Heathenry. When an individual declares for Theodish Heathenry he must understand that democratic procedures have no place in any aspect of Theodism. This is a cultural gap that one will face but one that must be understood if the individual is to gain from what Heathenry has to offer him."

So while all Theods are Tribalist, the latter does not hold true. One may be Tribalist without being Theodish. The difference is largely one of social structure and hierarchy.

Heathens do not meet in churches. Most gather in private homes or on private land. It is quite common for rites and celebrations to be held outdoors when weather permits. The most common name for a group of practicing Heathens is a *Kindred*. It may also be referred to as a *Mot*, if one is of Anglo-Saxon belief. Most of the kindreds and organizations out there fall somewhere along the spectrum of belief and practice mentioned previously, and understanding and application of Heathen thews[13] will vary accordingly.

Now, denomination aside, being Heathen is about more than worshipping the Norse Gods and Goddesses. Heathenry evolved as part of a cohesive culture. And while the natural evolution of that culture and religion was interrupted by 2,000 years of Christianity, there are specific cultural, social, and even linguistic patterns that are part and parcel of Heathenry. This is one of the things that differentiates indigenous traditions from Neo-Paganism and Wicca: They have a firm grounding in a specific culture, and with that culture comes a unique set of values, ethics, and a worldview and cosmology. While there is nothing at all wrong with being Norse Pagan or Wiccan, to truly be *Heathen*, one must do more than simply honor the Vanir or the Æsir. One must also adopt and live by some version of Heathen values and worldview. It is this, more than anything else, that draws the line between Heathens and Pagans. Heathenry isn't just a belief in a specific set of Deities; it is a folkway—a way of living, thinking, and making choices consistent with Heathen lore and thew. That thew may differ from denomination to denomination, but there is a consistency of culture and cosmology uniting them. And while most Heathens prefer to worship only the Norse Gods, I would go so far personally as to say it doesn't matter if a Heathen also honors non-Norse Deities in addition to the Norse, so long as the thews and values lie somewhere along the Heathen spectrum. The thews and values impact the community at a greater level than what goes on in one's personal devotions that are, when all is said and done, a rooftree issue.[14]

Interaction, education, and even sharing of rites and rituals between various denominations of Heathens, between Heathens and other indigenous religions, and even between Heathens and Wiccans and Neo-Pagans is a positive thing with the potential to enhance all involved. There is much that we can all learn from each other. The line must be drawn, however, when such intercourse is approached not from a desire to share knowledge or from a position of mutual respect, but from a sense of entitlement and cultural misappropriation. While most Heathens are ever-willing to share the broadest aspects of practice, and to explain Heathen lore, thew and beliefs, many may be unwilling to openly discuss the more catalytic aspects of personal experience—specific sacred traditions such as the Heathen magico-religious practices of seidhr, spae, and runemal—with those outside of their faith (or not in actual, practical detail, at any rate). They are unique to Heathen culture. They assist in maintaining the community's might, worth, and strength, and some feel they should not be approached in detail, outside of specific Heathen cultural and cosmological paradigms. Most are very aware of what was lost with the coming of Christianity to Northern Europe and guard their newfound traditions assiduously.

Regardless of denomination, modern Heathens strive to reconstruct the practices of their ancestors, drawing on their lore for inspiration. Maintaining this sacred link to the past is a very important part of Heathen belief today. In many respects, it is the lifeblood of the faith; mindfulness of that continuity and of the responsibility to forge yet another link in that never-ending chain is what forms the foundation of modern belief and practice.

Chapter 2

Cosmology

Heathen Cosmology is quite complex and rich in both symbolism and meaning. The majority of sacred stories are preserved in the *Poetic Edda* and *Prose Edda,* both dating from 13th-century Iceland. Remnants of the Heathen religion also survive in Anglo-Saxon histories and healing manuscripts, as well as the Icelandic Sagas. Current scholarship in the fields of archaeology, history, linguistics, and anthropology continue to increase knowledge of the pre-Christian world. This body of work comprises what modern Heathens refer to as "lore." It is from the lore that modern Heathens draw their inspiration for the reconstruction of their ancient faith. These stories are meant to be studied, explored, and meditated upon. They are not meant to substitute for personal gnosis; rather, they should enhance such things. The various stories may be interpreted on a variety of levels and provide insight into the nature of the Heathen Gods and one's own spiritual journey.

Modern Heathenry, as was the Heathenry of old, is a polytheistic religion. This means that Heathens believe in individual Gods and Goddesses, each with an independent nature and personality. Some modern Heathens believe that there is a common source to the Gods, rather like a tree with many individual branches. Other Heathens believe that each of the Gods is an individual entity and that there is no common source. Regardless, the Gods are not seen as archetypal figures or aspects, but as living, evolving beings in Their own right. They may choose to interact with humanity both directly and indirectly, and there are many stories in lore of the Gods taking an active hand in human affairs. Some of these sacred stories, such as the tale of the creation of the world, may seem fanciful, but their complex symbolism points to the interconnectedness of all living things, their common origin at the hands of the Gods and the cyclical nature of the natural world of which humanity is part.

According to the Eddas,[1] the world began with what amounts to a "big bang." In the beginning, there existed a great chasm called Ginungagap. Within this yawning void lay two worlds: Muspelheim, the world of raging fire, and Niflheim, the world of ice, fog, and stillness. Within Niflheim lay the well Hvergelmir, from which flowed 10 primordial rivers. For eons, these worlds spun within the primal void of Ginungagap in cosmic opposition to each other. Eventually, however, they began to draw closer and closer until they collided. From this elemental conflagration, life burst into being and the process of cosmic evolution began.

From the primordial ooze created by the steam, ice, fog, and heat there arose the first being: a proto-giant named Ymir. Ymir was born when the ice of Niflheim melted in the heat caused by the nearness of Muspelheim. Some scholars believe Ymir's name to be related to the Sanskrit word *yama*, meaning "hermaphrodite" or "hybrid," and his dual nature is further held forth in that he is the progenitor of both men and giants.[2] The giant race was descended from a man and woman brought to life from the sweat pooling in a sleeping Ymir's armpits, and from his legs came a son. Ymir wasn't the only primal being to emerge from this cataclysmic meeting of ice and fire. Where the 10 primordial streams in Niflheim congealed, Auðumla, a mighty cow, came forth. From her milk, Ymir drew his nourishment. Auðumla lived on salt, which she licked from the ice and brine of Niflheim. As Auðumla licked the salty brine—matter that was infused with the creative life force—a new being began to emerge. This was Buri. Unlike Ymir and his progeny, Buri was stately and handsome. Buri had a son named Bor, who married the giantess Bestla. (Like many creation stories, we do not know where these other giants came from if not from the body of Ymir.) From Bor and Bestla were born the first three Gods: Odin, Hoenir, and Loður. Sometimes They are called Odin, Vili, and Vé.

These three Gods slew Ymir. He was so vast a being that, when he was killed, the flow of his blood from the wound caused a great flood that killed all the giants, save for two: Bergelmir and his wife. From this couple, the race of Jotuns is descended. This ancient flood may help to explain the enmity with which the Jotun race consistently greets the Gods. From Ymir's body, the three Gods formed the foundations of the world. They shaped the land from his flesh, the seas and oceans from his blood, the mountains from his bones, and the various trees from his hair. Midgard, the world of men, was formed from his eyelashes, and his brains were fashioned into clouds. The race of dwarves was created when the Gods transformed the maggots that feasted on the remnants of Ymir's flesh into this new race of beings.

The Gods set the dome of Heaven (by some accounts, crafted out of Ymir's skull) over all that was, and saw that it was supported at each corner by a sturdy dwarf. Each of these dwarves bore the name of one of the cardinal directions: Austri (East), Sudri (South), Vestri (West), and Nordri (North). Sparks flying out of Muspelheim were gathered up by the Gods and set high in the vault of heaven to glimmer and gleam as stars. The Gods took Night, a dusky giantess, and set her, along with her son, Day, in the Heavens. Their individual passages across the sky set in motion the 24-hour cycle of day and night. Night drives a great steed named Hrimfaxi, and the spittle from this horse's mouth, as he flies across the heavens, forms morning dew. Day follows after his mother with his steed, Skinfaxi. The radiance from Skinfaxi's mane casts a shining light over all the land, heralding the dawn. Night also had a daughter, Jorð. Jorð was the body of the living earth, a Goddess in Her own right, and eventually became the mother of the God Thor.

The Gods further set the sun and moon on their celestial courses. The moon is personified as a God named Mani, and the sun as the Goddess Sunne or Sol. They are carried in their celestial journey in carts led by a boy and girl of the same respective names, who were the son and daughter of a man named Mundilfari. These children were so beautiful in his eyes that he had dared to name them "Mani" and "Sol," after the Moon-God and Sun-Goddess respectively. The Gods were offended by his hubris and snatched the children away, placing them in the service of their namesakes. As the God and Goddess ride across the sky, their carts are chased constantly and unceasingly by two giants who transformed into hungry wolves and who wish to violently rid themselves of the order the Gods imposed. At Ragnarokk, or so Heathen eschatology goes, these wolves will capture the celestial carts and devour the sun and moon, leaving the world in darkness.

In the end, the Gods did not stop with the creation of just Midgard. They set in order nine worlds in all, which were connected by a gleaming rainbow bridge called Bifrost:

1. Midgard, the world of men.
2. The pre-existing Muspellheim, the world of raging fire.
3. Niflheim, the other pre-existing world, of ice, cold, and stillness.
4. Asgard, the shining home of the Gods.
5. Vanaheim, the home of the Vanir-Gods (of whom we will learn more later in this chapter).
6. Jotunheim, the stormy realm of the giants.
7. Swartalfheim, the home of the dark elves.
8. Lightalfheim, the world of the light elves.
9. Helheim, home of the dead.

In addition to the Jotuns, there were other beings who interacted with the Gods as well. Light and dark elves each inhabited their own realm. In later Germanic folklore, they were associated strongly with nature spirits, vaettir, and even the spirits of the dead. These beings may or may not be favorable to mankind, depending on the circumstances of interaction and the nature of the person involved.

Two symbols hold a place of utmost importance in Heathen cosmology: Yggdrasil, or the World-Tree, and Urdabrunnr, the Well of Wyrd. The Gods are "integrally bound up with Yggdrasil and Urth's Well."[3] The Tree itself is the supporting axis of the multi-verse. It sustains life and being and supports the very fabric of existence. It is central to any understanding of the complexity and richness of Northern religion. Yggdrasil connects the worlds. It is the chief holy sanctuary of the Gods, their primary abode. There, by Urda's Well (another variation of *Urth's* Well), the Gods pronounce judgement every single day. In the "Griminismal" (a tale in the *Poetic Edda*), Odin refers to Yggdrasil as "the best of Trees." Traditionally it is seen as a great ash tree with branches rising higher than the eye can see, with immense girth and large, thick roots. Conversely, some envision it as a yew tree, and still other sources consider it to be part and parcel of every single type of tree that ever existed. Surprisingly, there is no indication that the Tree was created by the Gods. It, like the Nornir and the Well, is a thing out of time and space.

Yggdrasil supports the web of fate, woven by the Nornir, three wise women that oversee the Well and use its sacred waters to nourish the Tree. This is very important, because the Tree that supports all that is and all that will be is under attack. Yggdrasil has three mighty tap roots, each extending into one manifestation of the sacred well: one terminates in Niflheim, into the well Hvergelmir; one in Jotunheim, into the well of Memory, the well of the Jotun Mimir; and the final one into Urdabrunnr, the well of Fate. An ancient dragon, Nidhoggr, gnaws at the root beneath Hvergelmir. If the Tree topples, so will the fabric of the multi-verse. The Nornir prevent this however, daily pouring healing waters from Urda's Well over the body of the Tree. This water, containing the resolution of all things past and the impetus for all things to come, restores the Tree, healing its wounds.

The Nornir, the three mighty women who sit at the foot of Yggdrasil, are, like the Tree itself, beings out of time and space. Even the Gods Themselves must bow to the fate the Nornir decree. The first and most ancient of the Nornir is called Urd (Urda, Urða, Urth, Wyrd). She governs all actions that have passed and that have become set fate. The second Norn is named Verdandi, and She reflects the actual process of fate being made. She is the here and now. The third and youngest of the Nornir is named Skuld, and She governs what is to come as a direct result of the choices of the past. The Nornir will be discussed in more detail in Chapter 4. For now, suffice it to say that these three powerful beings govern causality and consequence, setting it in an order and rhythm that even the Gods must obey. These threads of decision and obligation are woven into a vast web of intertwining threads that connects everything and everyone.

Urda's Well, a bubbling stream, is the place where all fate, memory, and being resolve. Eventually the essence and energy of all fate and all choices flow into Urda's Well. It contains the ancestral, primal memory of all that was and the potentiality of all that will come to pass. The Well itself is a sacred enclosure, and the force that fills it is of holy manifestation. It may be considered to be the source of all holiness, wholeness, and health. As such, its waters possess magic beyond even that of the Gods. The Well and the Tree define and determine the nature of Northern cosmological thought in that they are both beginning and terminus for every action taken not only by mankind but by the Gods, as well.

Perhaps no other God is so strongly associated with Yggdrasil than Odin, the Allfather and foremost of the Gods. One of Odin's *heiti*, or sacred bynames, is Yggr: "The Terrible." The word *Yggdrasil* literally means "steed of Yggr." The World Tree was actually Odin's gallows; in search of power, Odin hung Himself on Yggdrasil, allowing it to carry Him beyond the realm of the living. He hung, wounded by His own hand, for nine days and nine nights until, in the midst of His agony, He was able to seize and win the runes. The runes are esoteric keys of transformative magic that allowed him to enchant the mind, raise the dead, turn the tide of combat, strengthen warriors, incite fear, heal the wounded, and bind the forces of chaos. The Tree is a doorway, as well as the means to pass through it. Odin's ordeal on the Tree shows this clearly and provides a cosmic counterpart for a powerful initiatory journey—one that has echoes in Shamanic traditions in many European cultures. One may speculate that the Tree arose out of the proto-mire of Ginungagap at the moment of the primal clash of worlds that brought about the creation of life. Therefore the Tree contains within itself that evolutionary drive, but there is no conclusive evidence in lore to support this theory.

After setting the worlds and multi-verse in order, the three Gods—Odin, Hoenir, and Loður—decided to create humankind. They took an ash and an elm, both sacred trees, and transformed them into the image of bodies, one male and one female. Odin gave them breath; Hoenir gave them consciousness and spirit; and Loður gave them blood, warmth, and actual life. As the first generations progressed, Odin Himself walked amongst the first people, teaching them right from wrong, establishing a system of ethics, and teaching them the fundamental skills they would need to prosper. Later stories tell how a God (some say Heimdall, some say Odin), disguised as a man named Rig, traveled the earth, siring children and teaching them runes, rulership, wisdom, and lore. The important thing to remember is that humankind is kin of the Gods, first crafted by Their own hands, then imbued with Their own lifeforce, and later descended directly from Them.

There are three mighty tribes of sacred beings: the Æsir (of which Odin, Hoenir, and Loður were the first), the Vanir, and the Jotun race.

Though not Gods specifically, the Jotuns often intermarried with the other Gods, and many of them were, thus, elevated. Traditional scholarship ascribes the venues of warcraft, knowledge, order, and justice to the Æsir; fertility, love, prosperity, and abundance to the Vanir; and chaos, destruction, and change to the Jotuns. The Jotuns, at best, are greeted with ambivalence by a majority of modern Heathens and, at worst, actively despised. The relationship between the Æsir and the Vanir did not start out on a pleasant note.

In another lay (tale) of the *Poetic Edda*, the Voluspa, the Seeress summoned to life by Odin speaks of the first war:

> "The first war in the world I well remember,
> When Gullveig was spitted on spear points
> And burned in the hall of the High God:
> Thrice burned, thrice reborn
> Often laid low, she lives yet.
>
> The gods hastened to their Hall of Judgement,
> Sat in council to decide whether
> To endure great loss in loud strife
> Or let both command men's worship.
>
> At the host Odin hurled his spear
> In the first world-battle; broken was the plankwall
> Of the God's fortress: the fierce Vanes
> Caused war to occur in the fields."[4]

From this we see that the Vanir and the Æsir, two powerful tribes of Gods, began a war over who would be most honored and receive the sacrifices of humankind. The war began with the attempted slaying of Gullveig. Some modern Heathens view Gullveig as a hypostasis of the Goddess Freya, with the threefold burning being a type of initiation into power. Others believe She is the Seeress Who Odin commands to life in the Voluspa. Still others see Her as simply another Vanic Goddess in Her own right. Gullveig's name translates as "gold-intoxication," and it is believed that Her presence among the Æsir so disrupted the structure and the order of their society, by the inciting of greed and hunger, that it was deemed necessary to kill her. It may also be that the type of magic possessed by the Vanir and embodied by Gullveig—a magic called *seiðr*, which involved glamour, mind control, and being filled with the intoxication of otherworldly forces—was seen as immensely dangerous by the Vanir. This latter theory may be called into question by the fact that Odin Himself later mastered the wielding of this system of power.

At any rate, Gullveig was slain by being burned in the Hall of the Gods three times, and three times She rose from the flames. This was so great an insult to an emissary of the Vanir, that it brought the two tribes of Gods to the brink of war. War was officially declared by the casting of Odin's spear over the opposing force, a custom which continued to be a declaration of warfare in Norse society. The battle was long and vicious, but neither side was able to gain victory. Eventually a truce was declared and, as was not uncommon in Norse society, hostages were exchanged to cement a pact of peace. These hostages would be integrated into the opposing society as full members serving as frith-weavers, or peace-weavers, and essentially making the two tribes kin. The Vanir sent three of Their mightiest Gods: Frey, Freya, and Njord (we will learn about them in Chapter 3) to the Æsir; the Æsir, in return, sent Odin's brother Hoenir and the wise Jotun, Mimir, friend (and by some accounts, uncle) to Odin. Initially, this didn't work out so well. Hoenir, though wise, was slow of speech, and the Vanir initially thought that they had been sent someone lacking in wisdom. They observed how Hoenir often sought council with Mimir and, in anger, decapitated the Jotun, sending His head back to the Æsir. Though grieved by this turn of events, the war was not renewed. Eventually the two tribes of Gods integrated as kin, and Mimir's head was restored to life by Odin's magic.

Northern Cosmology is unique in that it contains the concept of "destiny of the Gods," or Ragnarokk—a final battle in which the Gods will fight against the forces of entropy and destructive chaos led by Surt, the Lord of Muspelheim. Building up the army of Asgard in preparation for Ragnarokk is the driving motivation for Odin, and much of His knowledge seeking is done with this ultimate goal in mind. The beginning of that final cataclysmic battle will be heralded by the sound of Heimdall's horn. The God Heimdall stands on Bifrost bridge, ever-watchful for the first signs of this impending doom.

During Ragnarokk, the dead walk the earth; chaos, oath breaking, and violence will reign in the world of men:

> Brothers will fight and kill each other,
> Cousins will destroy kinship.
> It is hard in the world, much whoredom,
> An ax age, a sword age, shields are split,
> A wind age, a wolf age, before the world falls;
> No man will spare another.[5]

Yggdrasil finally falls prey to the gnawing of the dragon Nidhogg; Jotuns converge on Asgard, attacking the world of the Gods; and Loki is said to lead the forces from Jotunheim against the Gods. The sun and moon are finally captured and devoured by the wolves that chase them and many of the Gods fall in combat against Their foes: Odin is devoured by the wolf Fenris, and Freyr is slain by Surt. Heimdall and Loki die locked in mortal combat against each other. Thor is killed by the foul breath of the world-serpent, and the very foundations of the multi-verse crumble.

There is, however, rebirth after the destruction. The earth rises from the sundered sea, the children of the sun and moon take up their parents' mantle, and a man and a woman—Lif and Lifthrasir (Life and Stubborn Will to Live)—survive the carnage and live to re-propagate the earth. Many of the Gods actually survive; Hoenir lives, and a reference is made in the Eddas to His casting lots, which indicates that the sacred rites and rituals also survive. Balder returns from the land of the dead, as does His slayer, the blind God Hod. Thor's sons, Magi and Modi, survive, as do Odin's sons Vidar and Vali. The world is renewed, and Divine order reestablished.

It is not known how deeply Christianity affected beliefs about Ragnarokk. Nor is it known whether or not the Gods are able to prevent or avert this cataclysmic battle. But the multi-verse was created by a violent collision of opposing forces, and from that moment on, that battle against Ragnarokk was inevitable. It completes a cycle begun by the Gods' slaughter of Ymir and ordering of the nine worlds. Whether or not the Gods actually die in the way that man would understand it is unclear. The question of whether or not a God *can* die is best left to other theologians. In a way, the coming of Christianity to Europe was a type of Ragnarokk, but as within the sacred stories, the Gods survive and the religion is reborn. In the next chapter, we will explore the various Gods and Goddesses of the Northern pantheon.

Chapter 3

The Gods and Goddesses

In this chapter, the various Gods will be explored both from the perspective of lore and from that of personal experience. Various prayers and meditations will be provided to help the newcomer deepen his or her relationship to the Gods. It should be noted that everyone's experience with the Gods will differ, and one should avoid comparisons between oneself and how others may experience the same Deity. I have chosen to share some of my own personal experiences in this chapter, but readers should keep in mind that the Gods are individuals and Their relationship with each of us may differ just as our relationships with each other differ.

As noted in the previous chapter, there are three tribes of holy and/or supernatural beings: the Æsir, Vanir, and Jotun race. The largest family of Gods was called the Æsir. (The word *Ás* means "God" in Old Norse.) The Goddesses numbered amongst this tribe were called *Asynjur*. In the *Prose Edda*, it is stated clearly that the Goddesses and Gods were of equal power. As a collective group, the various tribes of Gods are occasionally referred to as the *Reginn* or "Ordered Powers." Foremost amongst the Æsir—indeed amongst all tribes of Gods—was the Allfather, Odin. We will begin with Him.

Odin (Woden)[1]

I will hail the bold God, Lord of Asgard's hosts.
I will praise the Lord of Valhalla.
I will celebrate His strength, cunning and wisdom,
This God of warriors and kings.
I will praise Him, the Allfather,
Husband of Frigga, Delight of Her arms.
I will hail the Drighten and Ring-giver,
Whose gifts inspire His chosen.
I will laud this Wooer of women,
Whisperer of charms and seduction.
I will sing of the Master of Poets,
Ensnarer of many an unwary heart.
I will raise a horn in His honor.
May victory be Yours, Valfaðr.
Hail, Woden! Hail the Wisest of Counselors![2]

Odin is a God of many names: Woden, Oðinn ("Fury" or "Frenzy"), Allfaðer (Allfather), Herjan (Lord), Wunsch (Wish-Giver), Yggr (The Terrible), Veratyr (God of Being), Fimbultyr (Mighty God), Hrjotr (Roarer), Svipall (Changeable), Gangleri (Wanderer), Hangagoð (God of the Hanged), Geirvaldr (Spear Master), Herteit (Glad of War), Glapsviðr (Seducer), Thekkr (Welcoming One), Sanngetal (Finder of Truth), Oski (Fulfiller of Desire), Sigfaðir (Victory Father), Grimnir (Masked One), Bolverk (Bale Worker), and Harbarðr (Greybeard), to name but a few.[3] The meaning of His primary name Odin, or Oðinn, is from the Old Germanic word for "berserker fury" and refers to ecstatic trance for Odin is a God of ecstasy, of the storm, of poetry, incantation, magic, battle, death, and transformation. At the same time, He is a God of wisdom, mental acuity, knowledge-seeking, and divine order. Some modern Heathens believe that the predominance of bynames, or heiti, was a product of the respect, awe, and even fear in which this God was held in pre-Christian Europe.[4] Be that as it may, the numerous praise names—more than 150 on record—certainly point to the many faces and guises this God was and is capable of taking. In fact, one of Odin's primary attributes was His tendency to disguise Himself as a common wanderer, to traverse freely through the nine worlds, gathering knowledge, furthering His plans, and interacting with mortals.

After the creation of the worlds, it was Odin who breathed life into the first man and woman. For this reason, as well as for His place in the pantheon, He is referred to as the Allfather, a paean to His life-giving power. Odin as Breath-Giver is tied indisputably with Odin as Father of Runes and Seeker of Knowledge. So many of His heiti invoke the power of the spoken word and the power of focused breath: Omi (One Whose Voice Resounds), Hvethrungr (Roarer), Vithrimnir (Contrary Screamer), Galdrafaðr (Father of Galdr), Gollnir (Shrieker), Eyluðr (Ever-Booming), and the list goes on. Odin is a God of magic and power. In magical practice, to speak is to call into being. A large part of rune magic was the chanting of special songs and the singing of runes (called *galdr*, meaning "to sing" or "to crow"[5]) to control the unfolding of being or sometimes to call and control spirits. Therefore, to speak is to imbue with life, a power belonging first and foremost to the Gods.

So as Breath-Giver, Odin imbues creation with the animating principle. He breathes life into our most hidden, secret dreams and unhoned talents. He awakens our passions, fires of inspiration, creativity, and occasionally ferocity within us. And He has the most annoying tendency to throw open doors long thought barred and sealed within the chambers of the heart. More than breath, from the Allfather comes awareness—a frightening gift at times. We are birthed by His exhalation, and therefore, at death, we are brought back to Him and into Him by His inhalation. Our lives are the span between two breaths of a God; not only does Odin give us life, but our lives begin and end with His breath.

Adam of Bremen, in the 11th century, declared, "Woden, id est furor" (Woden, He is fury).[6] Woden is certainly that, but even more, He is hunger. Throughout the corpus of our lore,[7] it is clear that Oðinn hungers for knowledge. He seeks and even subjects Himself to torture in order to acquire wisdom, knowledge, and understanding. The most notable and well-known example of this is recorded in the "Havamal," where the Allfather says:

I know that I hung on a windy tree
nine long nights,
wounded with a spear, dedicated to Odin,
myself to myself,
on that tree of which no man knows
from where its roots run.

No bread did they give me nor a drink from a horn,
Downwards I peered;
I took up the runes, screaming I took them,
Then I fell back from there.[8]

This recounts the tale of how the runes were won. The Allfather willingly sacrificed Himself, hanging on Yggdrasil, wounded by His own weapon, for nine days and nights of agony. On the ninth night, the runes surged into His consciousness. He spied them in the abyss below and seized them up triumphantly. This one event perhaps most clearly defines Odin's essential nature: the hunger to always go further and deeper.

Certainly this is not the only example in the Eddas of Oðinn's quest for knowledge. We see it again in the Vafðrudnismal, where (against the advice of the All-Mother Frigga), He ventures forth to challenge a wise and cunning giant to a test of riddles. Should He lose, the price would be His head. Of course Oðinn won, and it was the giant who forfeited his life. To gain the knowledge to use His power and wisdom wisely, Odin journeyed to the well of Mimir to barter for a draught of the magical elixer. The price for His drink was high: He was forced to tear out and sacrifice one of His eyes, which now lies hidden in Mimir's well. Then we have His winning of the sacred mead—the mead of poetry, inspiration, and creative fire. This mead, Oðroerir, initially belonged to the Gods and was made of their spittle and the ground up organic parts of the giant Kvasir. It was stolen from Them and eventually ended up in the hands of the Jotun Suttung. He locked it away in a cave and set his daughter Gunnloð to guard it. Oðinn disguised Himself as Bolverk and won the mead through guile, shapeshifting, and eventually through His seduction of Gunnloð, exchanging three nights of passion for three sips of the mead. From this union, the God of poetry, Bragi, was born.

This episode illustrates perhaps another of His most outstanding characteristics: the All-Father loves women—all shapes, all sizes, and all ages. (This is a fact easily supportable by even the most cursory reading of the Eddas! Take, for example, the Harbarðsljoð. While Thor boasts of Jotuns He has slain, Oðinn, disguised as Harbard, boasts of His sexual conquests.) He cherishes women, especially those who cherish Him in return. A word should be said about Oðinn's boasts of sexual conquest. I do not feel that such boasts on the part of a God are ones of betrayal or machismo. Rather they are an admission of a sexuality, energy, and vital force too powerful to be contained; a symbol of life, exuberance, and strength; and above all, an advocation of vitality and of seizing the moment in a life that is all the sweeter because it must seem so fragile, so threatened, to those Gods whose ears are constantly straining for the blast of Heimdall's horn. And for every person who opens to Him, who loves Him just a little, who is able to contain, for however short a time, a single drop of the enormity of His essence, more of Him is able to be in the world. We are doorways, vessels, windows for this most active of Gods.

Perhaps it is not surprising for a God so strongly associated with vital power, that we also find in Woden a God of healing, though this aspect of His nature was strongly suppressed during the Christian conversion of Scandinavia and Iceland. There are only three extant sources citing Odin as healer. The first is the Second Merseburg Charm, in which an injured horse is healed:

> Phol and Wodan rode into the woods,
> There Balder's foal sprained its foot.
> It was charmed by Sinthgunt, her sister Sunna;
> It was charmed by Frija, her sister Volla;
> It was charmed by Wodan, as he well knew how:
> Bone-sprain, like blood-sprain,
> Like limb-sprain:
> Bone to bone, blood to blood;
> Limb to limb—like they were glued.[9]

The second source is the "Nine Worts Galdr," from the Anglo-Saxon *Lacnunga* manuscript, which says:

> ...then Woden took up nine glory-rods, / struck the adder then so it flew apart into nine, / there apple ended it and its poison / so that it would never bend into a house. / Chervil and fennel, two of great might, / the wise lord shaped these plants / while he was hanging, holy in the heavens / he set them and sent them into the seven worlds / for poor and for wealthy, as a cure for all.[10]

The third source is the second rune charm from the "Havamal":

> "I know a second which the sons of men need, those who want to live as physicians."[11]

Of course, Woden also has His darker side. He is cunning, implacable, fierce, and brilliant in battle. He leads a host of the dead in the Wild Hunt and He possesses the power to command the dead to do His bidding.[12] Many of His heiti speak of His ability in combat: Herblindi (Host Blinder), Hnikuðr (Overthrower), and Valgautr (Slaughter God); others speak of His fury: Thror (Inciter of Strife), Woden (Fury), and Viðurr (Killer), to name but a few.[13] He is a Wanderer, wandering endlessly throughout the worlds in search of knowledge, wisdom, and some craft to hold Ragnarokk at bay and perhaps increase His own knowledge-hoard.

Morning Meditation Rite to Odin

Stand or sit before your personal altar.

Light a candle or perhaps a bit of incense; this provides a focus for the subconscious mind.

Begin to focus on your breath. Spend 5-10 minutes in a simple centering breathing: inhale four even counts, hold four, exhale four, and hold four counts, while focusing on all the life energy in your body gathering at a point about 2 inches below the naval.

Think on Yggdrasil, the sacred Tree that supports the multi-verse. Feel it strong and sturdy, with branches stretching up higher than the eye can see and roots, thick and mighty, plunging deep into the body of the earth. Feel yourself part of that Tree, connected to it in thought, drawing sustenance from it as it feeds its life-giving essence into all the worlds. Feel yourself rooted and strong as the Tree is rooted. As you exhale, feel all the energy gathered during your centering breath, plunging down and into the earth, connecting you to the body of Mother Earth, just like the roots of the Tree connect it to the source of its power. Spend 5 minutes consciously sending your vital force down into the earth with each exhalation, visualizing rich, sturdy roots.

Focus on your altar, and turn your attention to Woden. Breath Him in. Consciously take in His essence as you inhale, filling yourself with the vital force of this God. Feel it filling you, with each inhalation, from toes to crown. Feel that connection with Him, open and powerful. Feel all that He is reaching down, rooting you as the roots of the Tree steady its body.

Offer up the following prayer:

> Mot þa worda min muðes ond þa geondðenca min geðonces gelician þé, Leof min.
>
> [Pronunciation: *Mot tha worde min muthes ond tha yeondthenke min yethonkes yelikan the, Leof min*]

The translation would be, roughly, "May the words of my mouth and the contemplations of my heart be pleasing to Thee, My Beloved (Lord)." (Anglo-Saxon translation provided by Wulfgaest Thegn, Heah Blotere of the Haligwaerstow.)

Spend as much time as you would like basking in the presence of Woden, talking to Him, and meditating upon His attributes and His place in your life.

When you are finished say, "Woden, for all You are, I am grateful. Guide me this day."

Blow out the candle (or extinguish the incense) and go about your day.

Frigga (Frige)

> Shining Lady of Asgard,
> All-seeing, all-knowing,
> at Your command worlds are born,

at Your nod and tender smile, life bursts into being.
Valiant Goddess, ruthless foe, cunning Queen,
Illuminate our wyrd.
Strengthen our hamyngja.
Make us fruitful in all things, like the barley and flax
that is Your gift.
Nourish our souls, God-Mother,
Pour forth from Your cornucopia of abundance
and in return we will give You our devotion,
our praise, our industry.
Holy Mother of all life, foremost amongst the Asynjur,
bestow upon us Your wisdom.
Make our hearts fertile fields for Your bounty, and
on Your spindle of shimmering starlight,
weave for us a joyous fate.

As Odin is the All-Father, so Frigga is the All-Mother, Lady of Asgard. She is a great Seer, and it is said that She knows all fate but speaks it not. She lives in a great hall in Asgard called Fensalir, and Her chief companion among the other Goddesses is Her sister Fulla, who guards Frigga's treasure chests. Additionally, 11 other Goddesses serve as Her handmaidens and wise counselors. Though She does not travel about the various worlds like Her Husband, Frigga, too, takes a strong interest in human affairs and, on at least one occasion, sent her handmaiden Fulla to work Her will in the mortal world.

She is generally considered to be a Goddess of frith-weaving and right order. In many respects, Frigga is a power broker. Many modern Heathens tend to see Frigga as a Goddess of the household, but any pigeonholing of such a mighty being is, at best, ill-advised. In considering Frigga as Goddess of the household, it is important to look at what maintaining a harmonious home really entails. Do you want a home into which you can welcome your ancestors with pride (for within Heathenry, one's ancestors remain vital members of one's family)? Do you want a hearth that will reflect the bonds you have with those you love—a place to nurture heart and spirit in a way that far surpasses the simple provision of physical shelter? Such simple acts as cleansing one's personal space or creating a meal become acts of magic, the mindful crafting of a spiritual foundation and the cyclical renewal of reservoirs of wisdom and intent. These things then represent the unbending strength of ancestral knowledge flowing from one's own hands into everything and everyone touched. The home then reflects one's bond with the ancestors and willingness to contribute not only to the strength of loved ones but also to the line of knowledge that began with our foremothers. Frigga teaches us to make that connection. She also teaches us to reexamine female strength and power and shows us that femininity most definitely encompasses both virtues, for She is as formidable and fierce as any battle-tested warrior.

Frigga is also commonly seen as a Goddess of wisdom. The wisdom of Frigga is the wisdom of allowing one's wisdom and power to shine through in the small decisions, the smaller seemingly unimportant aspects of one's life, or the seemingly mundane. Establishing a home, for instance, becomes a thing of strength, reflecting devotion and connection to a line of knowledge and troth that will extend far beyond any one life. It becomes a thing of pride, reflecting one's love and openness to Divine presence. And it becomes a declaration of duty to kindred, and to the knowledge that what we do is not grounded in remote, arcane ritual but in the simplicity of our daily lives. In modern parlance, one might call Frigga the manager of Asgard, and as such, She is a Goddess of an almost military efficiency.

On a purely temporal level, think about what the proper running of a household involves: financial management, healing skills, the strategic forethought of a master general, the intuitive spiritual awareness of a mystic, and vigilance and diligence against disruption on every possible level. It isn't a "battle against dirt," but rather a battle against entropy. And Frigga, as Divine power broker, teaches us how to best utilize our resources in every aspect of our lives to most efficiently win this battle. As power broker, Frigga is a Mistress of Wyrd and Queen of Asgard (with all that entails to the Germanic mind). Many modern Heathens see a strong connection between Her and the Nornir and associate Her spinning of cosmic threads with the maintaining of Divine order.

My own personal experiences with Frigga have been most enlightening, and I will share them here. She is maternal, in a way, without being in the least motherly; Her presence has the most grounded and solid feeling of any Deity I have ever experienced. It is like the thick roots of some ancient yew stretching deeply enough into the earth that it will never be uprooted. Her presence is quiet; understated; strong, without being extroverted; firm, without any sense of what, in a mortal woman, would be self-aggrandizement. It is not the quiet of shy passivity at all, rather the concentrated knowledge of one's own skill and power. When Her presence is strong, it awakens in me the awareness of my own maternal lineage, of a powerful line of women stretching back into memory, and of experience patiently passed from mother to daughter through action and example. Over the years, Frigga has taught me how to accurately summon all of my resources to hand, of the necessity of domestic networking (a thing that would normally have occurred automatically through one's female relatives but that, in today's society, is fast becoming a forgotten art), and of assuming the position of leadership within the house—a position of accountability and responsibility for everyone and everything under one's roof.

With my love of the warrior arts, Frigga was kind enough to point out that the skillful warrior first puts herself beyond the possibility of defeat and only then looks for the opportunity of defeating her opponent.[14] That resilient clarity of purpose stems from having one's foundation firmly in order. The harmonious and swiftly functioning home is a reservoir of power that one can draw upon in times of stress and ever-increasing challenges. It is a place that should nurture the heart and fortify the spirit.

Under Frigga's guidance, creating a welcoming home has thus become synonymous with creating a welcoming heart and with keeping the metaphorical door open to any of the Gods or Goddesses. It is, again, that special quality of mindfulness, an awareness of one's interconnectedness to one's kindred and community, an awareness of the world around us. It involves a willing sharing of the journey and all the gifts found therein, even if that means occasionally causing conflict to spur one's growth.

Industriousness has become far more than simple plodding repetition of necessary tasks; it has become, to me, the process of constantly striving to develop one's gifts and the quality of excellence within one's self. It entails accepting the responsibility to do your life's work as Deity defines it, even if that means getting up and cleaning the kitchen! It is also the responsibility of being productive with one's knowledge and of taking pride in doing the smallest tasks well. There is something very contemplative in Frigga, yet it is a contemplation forged in swift action. When my hands are covered with Hers, guided by Her, even the most mundane task becomes a prayer, an act of reverence and thanks.

I have glimpsed vestiges of Frigga as Queen of Asgard, remote and awe-inspiring. I have certainly in my seiðr work glimpsed Her spinning strands as thick with magic as any that flow from the hands of the Nornir. As Odin is Allfather, I know that Frigga is Allmother. However, it is not in any such grand way or form that I have been most touched by Her. She chose to come in as wife and hearth-keeper and, by sweeping away those things that were most stunting my growth, opened my eyes to the preciousness of my Kindred, my home, and those I love. What I had once been so quick to disregard I now would defend with my life at blade's edge, if need be. I have come to see Frigga as defender of the home, in its broadest sense, and have often had cause to thank Her for Her unerring patience.

Meditation for Frigga

This is a mirror meditation. Have a small mirror into which you can gaze, perhaps resting in a circle of candles. There should also be a set of runes available. I have found that candlelight seems to act as a trigger for the unconscious mind. If you wish, you may set up an altar to Frigga or make offerings. Frigga shines in every woman and impacts the wyrd of every man. Everyone, male or female, has a connection to Frigga. She is the Allmother and can teach us much about strength and hallowing of the self. Gazing into the mirror, reflect on how Frigga manifests in you and which path of Her you most strongly allow to come through. Where do you block Her? What is your understanding of Her? What do you feel She most has to teach you? After 10–15 minutes of silent meditation, each person should draw a rune, which he or she will meditate on for the next seven nights. This is a gift from Frigga, a drop of Her wisdom.

Thor (Thunor)

I raise a horn to Thor the Mighty.
Glad I am to call Him friend.
He fiercely protects those He loves.
He watches over the weak and the innocent.
He is kind and gentle, this God, and wise—
Wise enough to save his daughter through a battle
of wits.
He is loyal to His family; He does not question
their affections.
He is strong but not overly prideful. What other God
would masquerade as a woman,
to reclaim his most sacred weapon—all for the good
of His tribe? What other God would willingly bear
the company of Laufey's son, even though He must
know this brings as much trouble as boon?
He is friend to all, caring and gentle. His strength
nourishes, heals, and reclaims that which is wounded.
He is sure and grounded, as sturdy as the roots of the
sacred Tree. He hallows with His presence. He makes
that which is sundered hale, healthy, and whole.
I praise You, Son of Odin, Son of Jorð. Husband of Sif,
Father of Magni and Modi.
I hail You, strong defender of those You love, warder of
all Your younger kin.
Hail, Thor.

Perhaps no other God is so well loved by Heathens both ancient and modern as the God Thor. He was very likely the most widely worshipped of any of the Heathen Gods throughout pre-Christian Northern Europe. He is the God of the common man, seemingly uncomplicated and down-to-earth. He is the defender of mankind, warding the world against the incursion of the forces of chaos and destruction. He hallows by His might and by His very presence, and today Heathens wear the symbol of His mighty hammer Mjolnir ("Crusher") as a sign of troth. He girds the world against its own dissolution. His is the power to restore holiness and wholeness to anything He touches. For this reason, a hammer was laid in the bride's lap at the wedding feast to ensure the fertility of the couple—a custom that continues today among modern Heathens. Thor is a God of wholeness, well-being, and protection.

Thor is kind, just, and very protective of those He cares about: His wife Sif, His daughter Thruð (strength), and His sons Magni and Modi (the Strong One and the Angry One). He is constantly fighting to ensure the security of His clan and extended family of the Gods so much so that He is primarily known for His ability at fighting Jotuns who constantly seek to undo what the Gods have wrought. In many respects, it is Thor's power that defines the inangarð. The concept of *inangarð* and *utgarð* is essential to any definition of the holy in Heathen culture. The community, clan, and tribe were viewed as the *inangarð*, a sacred enclosure protected against the forces of entropy and destruction represented by the *utgarð*. To hallow something is to bring it within the boundaries of the inangarð. Properly maintaining the integrity and wholeness of the inangarð (for instance, by proper behavior and by proper ritual performance and sacrifice) was crucial to maintaining the luck and strength of the tribe. Anything that threatened that order was dangerous and, therefore, of the utgarð. From this evolved the concept of *thew*, or tribal custom/law, which ensured that the strength of the inangarð would not be threatened by its own people. Thor constantly crossed into the untamed wilds of utgarð to slay those who threatened the peace of the Gods. In fact, He is the only God that does not use some mechanism to cross between worlds. Most use the bridge Bifrost, but Thor is too heavy so He cannot. Others utilize magical falcon cloaks or vehicles such as Freya's chariot. Thor needs none of that. His holy might is so powerful that He is able to wade through the proto-fabric of time and space on His own.

Thor will go to any lengths to protect His people, including temporarily sacrificing His masculinity! In one of the Eddic tales, Thor's hammer is stolen by a Jotun who will only return it if the Goddess Freya promises to be his bride. Well of course, Freya is not about to consent to any such bargain, so Thor (with Loki as His cunning attendant) dresses in women's clothing, disguising Himself as the Goddess, and tricks His way (with Loki's sly mind and words to help pave the way) into the Jotun's hall—ostensibly for the marriage feast. Once there, of course, the hammer is placed in His lap to hallow the "marriage," and that is the end of the Jotun and his kin.

In many ways (though this is a controversial and by no means readily accepted theory[15]), Thor fulfills the function in Asgard that a traditional Shaman would in a tribal community: He maintains the wholeness, health, and holiness of the community, and He protects it from otherworldly intruders and regularly travels between worlds. On at least one occasion, He cross-dresses, and He is regularly in the company of what may be seen by some as a "trickster" being (Loki). Whether one agrees with this or not, it is at least apparent that there is more to Thor than initially meets the eye.

The Strength of Thor: A Meditation

The strength of Thor is the strength that girds the world against destruction. The strength of Thor is that which contains the holy; it defines the inangard. The strength of Thor is the supporting vessel into which the Gods may pour Their Divine Maegen. Born of earth, He centers, grounds, and gives stability to that which is tenuous. He roots Midgard firmly within the multi-verse; He brings to life that which lacks vigor. He centers us in the NOW. He shows us the vitality of the moment. The strength of Thor is perseverance. It is fire and thunder, lightning and quake. He is His mother's son and the pride of His father.

Fierce, He protects the lowly, the trembling, the fearful. He hallows that which connects the generations and, with His wife, blesses Asgard, filling it with the flower of Their power. Dignity and pride, the might to defend, a forward faring spirit, cherisher of kin—this is the strength of Thor. He is shield and protector. He is companion and friend. His are the pillars that mark the frithstead. The strength of Thor does not yield in the face of loss and grief. It does not flicker away in the face of helpless vulnerability. The strength of Thor is the might of the hammer crushing the foe, but it is also the strength of compassion and care. The strength of Thor will nourish and comfort when all other comfort is lost. He strengthens the spirit and wards the soul against despair. He is the spine that supports us, often forgotten. And He never fails.

His pride is in His kin, and He battled for Thruð against the dwarf's incursion, His wit lying hidden beneath practical facade. His dignity was a small sacrifice to salvage His might when women's clothes He wore, and victorious He returned having vanquished the Jotun. He needs no vessel to cross the seas of wyrd and formless space. He stands in the liminal, making it physical and doing what must be done. He is unassuming yet mighty, a God for every man. His hammer is folk-binding—the emblem of His nature. It defines us, inspires us, and calls us to courage. It is the victory of Asgard over entropy and chaos. It rivets the fabric of being and binds us away from all harm.

Lover of Jarnsaxa, the iron-hearted; husband to Sif and defender of Her honor; Companion to Loki on many travels; bane of the Jotnar, who remain ever fearful. Warder of the Gods' halls, with many names, some very telling: Donar, Thunar, Asa-Thor, God of Thunder known to the Romans, son of Odin, beloved of the people. Called for healing, called for protection, called for insight, His wisdom held fast. Midgard's warder, God of the Country; Thrudugr, the Mighty; Thrudvald, Strong Protector; Father of Might and of Righteous Wrath; brother to Meili; Thrudvaldr Goda; Friend of Man; Giant-killer; Champion of Midgard—these names we remember.

Hail to Thor and the strength of His hammer. Hail to His insight and His willingness to aid. Ever the friend of those in need, ever the shield of those afraid.

Sif (Sibb)

I am the seed, lost in ignorance and fear.
Encompass me in the nurturing darkness
of Your rich soil. Let my roots drink deeply
from the nectar of wisdom that You offer.
Let me appreciate each day and hour of my journey,
each moment of my blossoming faith, for each step I take,
though difficult, brings me closer to You.

Let me treasure the time I must spend nurturing
my awareness
of Your bounty and grace. Let me feel the
gentle comfort
of Your patient guidance. I seek to grow in faith,
in knowledge of You,
the lessons of the passage of time etched upon
my toughening skin,
the tales of my survival by Your grace engraved
upon each withering leaf
of the days and nights of my existence.
Teach me to craft, in gentle service, a home
within my heart that will be an honor to You.
Let me never hesitate to invite You
into the home that is my heart.

Sif hallows. As Her husband, Thor, girds and wards hallowed space, so She sanctifies it within. She helps us maintain the holy. At least that is what I myself have learned from honoring Her, though it is not written in any body of surviving lore. My experience of Her has been that She makes things hale and whole. And that is no small gift; for the contemplative, it is perhaps the greatest gift of all. She helps us maintain integrity of spirit. She is a Goddess of both hallowing and harvest.

Sif is not mentioned much in the Eddas. When She is mentioned, it is usually as a corollary to Thor. She is known as the wife of Thor, mother of Their daughter Thruð (strength), and mother to the God Ullr (though Thor is not His father). One interesting mention of Her in the prologue to Snorri Sturluson's *Poetic Edda* refers to Her as a prophetess. She is also mentioned in various lays of the *Edda*: In the "Skaldskaparmal," She is coveted, along with Freya, by the giant Hrungnir. In the "Harbarddsljod," Odin accuses Sif of having a lover, which may of course simply have been to further harass Thor. Loki repeats this accusation in "Lokasenna," naming himself as the erstwhile lover.

The most famous mention of Sif, however, involves Her long, beautiful, golden hair. Loki sneaks into her bedchamber one night and crops it off, infuriating Thor and shaming His wife. Of course the trickster replaces it with hair forged of real gold, the only way to escape a beating by Sif's irate husband. Many modern Heathens accept the idea that her hair represents the grain crop (particularly wheat) and that this story may be symbolic of the seasonal harvest: the grain, so necessary for life, is cut and grows anew with the turning of the seasons.[16] Marion Ingham[17] points out that the few scholars who still support such nature-symbolism point to the fact that it is virtually indispensable to have thunderstorms for the grain to ripen—it fixes the nitrogen. And Thor with His mighty hammer is associated with thunder. Sif is to the inner what Thor is to the outer: One who hallows and girds against that which would destroy our center.

It is difficult to get a complete picture of Sif's nature from the fragments surviving in our lore. In another account, in the "Lokasenna," Loki was angered because He hadn't been invited to a feast of the Æsir, in breach of an oath by Odin that He would never accept drink at a feast unless it was also offered to His blood brother, Loki. In this instance, Sif appears as peace-maker, offering Loki a horn of mead and trying to still His anger. In fact, there is a strong connection between Sif and Loki in the surviving lore. He is the one that stole away her shining glory. I do not think that Her apparent grief over the loss of Her hair reflects simple vanity. Rather, I believe Her hair was an outward manifestation of Her inner power and strength. Loss of Her hair was, therefore, analogous to Thor's loss of His hammer. Everything surrounding Sif speaks of vital energy and strength: Her daughter's name; Her husband; her sons; and even Thruðheim, "Home of Power," the dwelling wherein She lived. Therefore, the shearing of Her hair, the symbol of Her own strength, would be a metaphor for a loss of power. She added to the strength of Her hall. Germanic culture often ascribes to women a certain holy power. This is evident from our earliest lore, when Tacitus comments on the immense regard given to certain prophetesses such as Veleda. Sturluson does refer to Sif in similar terms, naming Her as a seeress. In this way, one might speculate that it was *worth* She brought to Thor's house.

Taking that a step further, Sif may be the perfect Goddess to work with when learning to maintain and increase our own worth. Given that She was able to gain remuneration for the offense done to Her, by working through others (Thor threatening Loki who went to the dwarves who crafted Her hair), She may also have much to teach us about making and maintaining alliances. Furthermore, as Her son Ullr is named by Sturluson as a good one to call upon in single combat, so perhaps is His mother a good one to call when seeking remuneration or wergild for one's hurts. In our lore, the Goddesses are reckoned equal to the Gods in power. This could be taken to imply that Sif is Thor's equal in power, which would make Her a mighty Goddess indeed.

Centering Meditation for Sif

(Note: The chakras are not a Norse or Anglo-Saxon concept, but I have found them very useful in meditations of this type.)

Find a comfortable position. Sit quietly and begin to focus on your breath. Feel it flowing through your body, flowing through each and every part of you. As you inhale, feel yourself being filled with living energy; let it flow through you. As you exhale, feel it cleansing you of any tension, any negativity. Inhale slowly, evenly...exhale, feeling the energy cleansing you. With each exhalation, feel yourself relaxing; feel yourself sinking deeper and deeper into the flow and pull of your breath.

As you breathe, begin to focus on your root chakra. This is located in the perianal area. It is the place of our strongest connection with the earth, the channel through which we take in raw, passionate, survival energy. It is our link to the source of life, and to the center of the earth, the roiling fire of creation.

As you breathe, allow your consciousness to flow to the root chakra. With the gentle impetus of your breath, feel the root opening, filling with the lava, the churning, roiling energy that lies buried in the center of the earth. As you breathe, it becomes a burning, flaming orb of that chaotic life energy, one with the very core of the earth. With each exhalation, that fire burns brighter, hotter, connecting you in an unbreakable bond to the earth itself.

Now, allow your consciousness to move from the root, to the sex chakra. This is located roughly 3 inches below the naval. This is not only the seat of sexuality, but of our body consciousness and our emotional boundaries. As you breathe, feel the energy of your breath moving from the fire of the root, that central burning life-core, to the steadiness of the dark, moist earth that surrounds it. As your root is filled with the roiling fire of the earth's core, so that fire is contained in the dark soil surrounding it, and that black earth fills the sex chakra. As you breathe, feel its steady coolness enervating this chakra, connecting you even more strongly with the earth. As you breathe, feel that cool steadiness surrounding you, flowing through the sex chakra.

Now, move your consciousness to your solar plexus, located at the bottom of the sternum. Feel the energy, the primal awareness, moving from the sex chakra to the heat of the solar plexus. This is the seat of the will, the manifestation of the power first tasted at the root and nurtured at the sex. As you breathe, allow that life energy to fill the solar plexus. Feel the solar plexus expand, until your breathe is like the hot wind across the deserts. The solar plexus is alive with desert sands, hot wind, focused breath. As you breathe, allow this chakra to pulse in time with your breathe, radiating with the power of sun, sand, and heat.

Now move your consciousness to your heart chakra. This is the seat of growth and compassion, loss, love, joy, and pain. As you breathe, feel this chakra come alive. See it bursting green and strong—grass shooting forth from the earth, trees, plants, shrubs...life and creation blossoming. As you breathe, envision your heart as an endless expanse of forest, mountain, grass, flowers, fields, and plants. It is a sacred sanctuary of life, creativity, and being. As you breathe, allow this chakra to pulse in time with that breath, radiant and whole.

Now, move your attention to your throat chakra. This is the place from which all communication flows. As you breathe, feel that chakra expand until it becomes the broad expanse of the oceans, ebbing and flowing with each exhalation. Feel its cool comfort, the confidence of the primal oceans. With every breath, the tides move and the chakra opens. With each breath, you are connected more and more strongly to the cool comfort of the waters.

Now, move your consciousness up to the third eye, between your brows. With each breath, this chakra expands and begins to shine and glow like the sun. As you breathe, that light grows brighter; the nurturing warmth of the sun blazons forth from your brow. With each breath, feel the warmth and light growing stronger; feel the chakra opening wider, connecting you to the heavens.

Now move your consciousness to your crown. This is your connection to Divinity. As you breathe, feel your awareness of this chakra open until within this chakra flows the expanse of the universe. A thousand galaxies pulse and dance within this chakra. With every breath, feel the energy flowing from the fiery core of the root, through your body, up to the crown, connecting you to the endless expanse of the heavens. As you inhale, draw energy up from that burning core, through your chakras. As you exhale, feel it bursting from the crown, illuminating and reaching up toward the heavens. Continue to breathe, resting secure in the subtle play of physical energy.

Now, inhale drawing energy from the heavens, in through the crown. As you exhale, allow it to flow through the third eye, throat, heart, solar plexus, sex chakra, and down into the root, connecting you again strongly to the earth. Continue to breathe, focusing on allowing your energy to flow deeply into the earth, uniting you with its burning core, uniting you with the endless source of all life energy.

Now focus on your breath. Begin to inhale four counts, hold four counts. Exhale four counts, hold four counts. (Continue this until you are firmly grounded.)

Idunna/Iðun (Edgeongan)

Holy Idunna,
You see such promise in each tender seed.
Every vein of every leaf has been tenderly
drawn and creased by Your caring hands,
every petal of every living blossom
gently parted by Your deft fingers.
Would You then ignore the hearts of Your children?
We are scarred, and we are scared.
We push and we strive—wanting, needing,
rushing through the sacred moments of our lives.
We never see Your blessings; we never see the blessed
    synchronicity with which You fill our lives.
Such care, such joyful simplicity, is so very foreign to us.

Teach us, Goddess, to treasure those things
You so lovingly place within us.
We miss so much in our mad, mad rush away
from all that is precious within ourselves.
Teach us, Goddess, to cherish the littlest blessings
in our lives
So that when we finally pass from this world
We may pour forth these delicate jewels of memory
Into Your waiting hands.

Idunna is the Goddess who maintains the youth, vitality, and health of all the Gods. She does this by the gift of Her apples of immortality. Her name translates as "the Renewer," and that is precisely what She does. By some accounts, She is strongly connected to Yggdrasil and its primal power.[18] It is because of Her rejuvenating power that Loki was blackmailed into stealing Her away and delivering Her to the giant Thjiazi. Of course, She was later rescued—by Loki, in fact—and returned to the Æsir, but this story gives hints of how deeply Her power was coveted by the Jotuns. It is interesting to note that the giants coveted Idunna, not Her apples. The apples were useless unless they were given directly from Her hands as the regenerating power lay in this Goddess Herself.

The very first image I ever had of Idunna was that of a medieval virgin caught in the Unicorn tapestries, as indisputably bound and imprisoned as the unicorn she sought. For reasons that I am still unable to fathom, Idunna brought to mind images more befitting some Troubadour serenading the courts of the Acquitaine than proper Eddic lore. It was only once I truly began developing a relationship with Her that my preconceptions rapidly fell away. Now when I meditate on Idunna, my mind is flooded with images both exquisite and precise in their beauty but never, ever, passive. In Her, I see life and growth, endless and implacable. I see elemental union exploding in a vibrant tapestry of birth. I see a hand—sometimes delicate, sometimes ancient and withered—tracing the fragile vein-work of a single leaf, the fingers playing over the quivering green body, weaving it into life even as the Nornir weave the strands of our existence into being. I feel the sharp, aching poignancy of seasonal shift and change: one world withering to birth a new. For to me, Idunna is a Goddess of cycles and seasons, of ever-returning renewal and birth. Gentle in Her presence, She is everywhere, Her fingers caressing everything, urging life.

She connects what would not necessarily be united in our minds. I can easily envision Her deft fingers smoothing over the raw, knotted places on our life-skeins, gently coaxing those threads to bloom anew in unexpected ways. I believe there could be a very potent sexuality about Idunna, but I have not yet seen that aspect of Her nature. I catch glimpses of it in the urgency with which life is brought into being by Her hands. I have often experienced Idunna extending Her hand to the Goddess Hel, completing a cycle, creating union. As she brings life, so She honors and makes sacred death, the two being easily balanced in Her ever-serene hands. My student would say that Idunna gives to Hel, Who gives to Idunna, Who gives to Hel, and so forth, in never-ending cycle. Both nurture "deathing" and rebirthing. What Hel does below the surface (and that can be taken quite symbolically, as far as the spiritual journey and our unconscious resistance to growth is concerned), Idunna does above. Idunna is the surface of the earth, growing from the surface, reflecting all that Hel cherishes so deeply below in a very synergetic partnership.

Idunna is not a Goddess who surrenders easily to the pull of spiritual entropy and, though Her struggles may rest veiled under a disarming cloak of apparent passivity, I liken that aspect of Her Divine nature to the state of *zanshin* so celebrated and sought by martial artists—that place of utter stillness and spider-like awareness wherein everything is possible. I bring Idunna offerings of seeds, of all different types. Seeds are the quintessential symbol of initiation, for a seed symbolizes that knife-edge moment before concentrated potential bursts into being.

I would also call Her a Goddess of healing in that She has the ability to make sacred the most wounded parts of our spirits. She is a Goddess of the rhythms not only of evolution but of devotion. In whatever keeps one's spirit and heart pure, in whatever tends the gentle bud of hope, however delicate, there is Idunna. I find it interesting that Loki plays such an important role in the story of Her kidnapping for I would say that Idunna, like Loki, brings the gift of change, perhaps in a far gentler manner than the Sly One, but She brings it nonetheless. There is much in that connection between Loki and Idunna, however tenuous it may be by the standards of lore that begs further exploration.

Perhaps Her greatest gift is that of simplicity. I have come to believe that what She desires most of all is a mind and heart attuned to rhythms of devotion—attuned and therefore open to the planting of those spiritual seeds that are Her most cunning gift. *That* is Idunna, to me. That is the experience that I have been blessed to have at Her hands.

Bragi (Brego)

Husband of Iðunn, I hail You.
Your tongue is carved with runes of power,
And your mouth has become a gateway
of living inspiration. Words of beauty and
fate-weaving force
pour from Your lips like pearls from an
overflowing treasure hoard.
Son of Gunnloð, Son of Oðinn,
I praise Your poetic skill.
Hail, Bragi; I raise this horn to You.

Bragi is the progeny of Odin and the giantess Gunloð, conceived during the three nights of sexual pleasure given by Odin to Gunloð when He won back the sacred mead of inspiration and ecstasy. He is the husband of the Goddess Idunna and named by Odin as the "best of Poets."[19] Poets were powerful figures within Germanic society. They were liminal figures, capable of weaving fate with their words, of passing judgements and prophesying, and of being the active voice of various supernatural beings (that is, Gods).[20] They were visionaries capable of shaping the fabric of society and the luck of the tribe by the outpouring of their words. They ensured that the deeds of the tribe would be remembered, creating a visceral tie between the strength and might of one's ancestors and the potential deeds of living members of the community. They were a living bridge between past and present, and as such, Bragi holds a place of immense importance amongst the Æsir. It is fitting that He would be the progeny of Odin, Who is Himself a God of poetry, ecstasy, and inspiration.

Like the traditional role of the Shaman in many cultures, among the Norse, it was the poet's duty to open doorways of consciousness through which the Gods could speak. Through being imbued as they were with the gift of ecstatic inspiration (and sometimes revelation?), their words elevated their entire community.

Tyr (Tiw)

I will hail the grey God
Who walks in places neither light nor dark.
I will hail the One
Who holds duty to tribe and clan,
even above the binding vow of His sworn word,
in vanquishing the outlander.
I will hail Him who bears the sword as His symbol:
decisive, ruthless, just.
I will praise Him who sees what must be done
and quietly completes his duty.
He asks for neither praise nor glory,
boasts not with mighty words in the Hall.
He asks nothing but stands firm, steering His way
clearly through murky waters.
He is mighty, this God,
His glory found in His sword and the hand He
sacrificed.
I will hail Him as He faces the wolf, this warrior
Who betrays
for honor's sake.

Tyr is most well known for the binding of Fenris. Fenris was the son of Loki by the giantess Angurboða and had the shape of a huge, hungry wolf. At first, Fenris was welcomed (albeit with some trepidation) by the Gods, but eventually a seeress foretold that He would be the death of Oðinn at Ragnarokk. After that, the Gods decided to bind Him so that He could wreak no harm (not wishing to kill the son of one of Their own). They took Fenris to an isolated clearing and proposed a test of His strength, promising to undo Him if any of the bonds held. They tried to bind Him with every manner of fetter, but none would hold, for the wolf was quite strong. Finally, the dwarves crafted a rope as thin and delicate as a ribbon. They called it *Gleipnir* ("Open One") and crafted it from things as impossible to conceive as the sound of a cat, the beard of a woman, the spittle of a bird, the roots of a mountain, the breath of a fish—all things that do not really exist. Fenris suspected treachery when He saw how delicate the cord was and only agreed to be bound if one of the Gods would place His right hand, His sword hand, into the wolf's jaws. Of Them all, only Tyr stepped forward to do so. When Fenris first came to the Hall of the Gods, Tyr was the one who fed and cared for Him. Once Fenris truly realized that the Gods had no intention of releasing Him, He snapped off Tyr's hand at the wrist. Tyr is known therefore for His bravery in defense of His clan.

He is generally considered to be a God of warriors, and one of the Eddic rune charms suggests carving His rune, the rune tiewaz (shaped like an upwards pointing arrow) on one's sword for protection and victory in battle. He is also a God of justice and law, right action and thew. There is ample evidence that, long before Oðinn became Allfather, Tyr ruled the worlds as Skyfather. His name is certainly "cognate to Dyaus of Vedic myth and the elder Dyus Pater of Rome and Zeus of Greece, the Skyfather and progenitor of Creation."[21] By the time of the Eddas however, He had become known as Oðinn's son (or according to one Eddic lay, the son of a Jotun Hymir) and a Patron of Warriors. He is also Patron of the Thing, the legal assembly in Germanic cultures through which disputes were settled by law or holmgang.[22]

Lord Dan O'Halloran, a devout Tyrsman, speculates that "Tiw is less about conflict of 'war' and more about the mechanics of *recht* (right) and thus the resolution of conflict, a juridical function" and as such is concerned primarily with "clear resolution, honor and the preservation of thew."[23] One might say that Tyr is a God strongly involved in right action (despite any consequences to the self), just government, legal structure and decisions, societal order, and proper maintaining of healthy customs. He is a God of valor, courage, integrity, wisdom, and of course, martial prowess—particularly that of knowing when and how to fight.

Frigga's Handmaidens

The next 12 Goddesses are numbered in the retinue of Frigga. Traditionally, They are considered Her handmaidens, but a word should be said about this appellation: It is in no way derogatory. Each of these 12 Goddesses is powerful and independent in Her own right. The term *handmaiden* merely indicates that She is a trusted companion of the Allmother, more closely connected to Her than other Asynjur.

Fulla

Wise Goddess, Fast Friend of Frigga,
I raise this horn to You.
Keeper of secrets, keeper of mysteries,
Overseer of all undiscovered wealth,
I praise You for Your wisdom.
Trusted companion of the Allmother,
Mighty Goddess in Your own right,
I hail You.
Bring forth the mysteries within my own soul.
Nourish the treasures within me.
Teach me to find the power within myself
and to hold fast to my own secret strength.
Speak not of my weaknesses as I struggle to
overcome them,
as You speak not of the Allmother's plans.
Hail, Fulla, Goddess of stones.

Fulla is a very mysterious Goddess. She is mentioned specifically in the Merseburg Charm as Frigga's Sister. Her name means "bounty" or "plenty," and this may mean that She is a Goddess of hidden wisdom and hidden wealth, both actual and symbolic. She is said to be the Keeper of Frigga's treasure chest. This is no small duty. In Norse culture, the Lady of the house kept the keys to the wealth of the house, managed all aspects of the homestead, and provided wise counsel to the men. Only the Lady would have access or power to dispense the household wealth. To be entrusted with the wealth of the house was an immense responsibility and showed an incredible degree of trust on the part of Frigga.

It may be inferred that Fulla acted as Frigga's trusted counselor, for Sturluson notes in the *Prose Edda* that She shares the Allmother's secrets. Not only does She share Frigga's secrets, but She also often collaborates in Her plans. In the "Grimnismal," it tells that Frigga and Odin had each fostered a boy and wished to determine which one was the better man. Geirod was Odin's fosterling. It was Fulla who sent the message to King Geirod warning Him about Odin and turning His mind against the Allfather (Who was planning to visit in disguise). When Odin arrived, disguised as an old wanderer, He was hung between two raging fires for eight days and nights by the king, an act that later resulted in Geirod's death. So it seems Fulla is as wise and cunning as Her Sister.

Fulla is mentioned several more times in the lore. She is pictured as a lovely maiden with long, flowing hair held back by a band of gold. In poetic kenning, gold might be referred to as "Fulla's snood." There is a lovely prayer in the *Gisla saga Surssonar* offered by the hero shortly before his death:

> "My Fulla, fair faced, the goddess of stones
> Who gladdens me much, shall hear of her friend
> Standing straight, unafraid in the rain of the spears."

Meditation Activity to Honor Fulla

This is a meditation rich in symbolism. The object is to create a reliquary box that may be used both for further meditations on Fulla and as a representation of Her wisdom on one's personal altar. Before this meditation rite begins, gather a pretty box, preferably one with lock and key, and a plethora of objects that represent things that are important to you in your life—things that you cherish, things that bring you closer to the Gods, things that nourish you emotionally and spiritually, things that strengthen your spirit.

Begin by setting up an altar to Fulla. This is a powerful way of calling on and connecting to a Deity (altar work will be discussed in more detail in Chapter 9). Anything that speaks of the sacred to you can go on a personal altar. Once your altar is complete, hallow the space and sit down in front of it. Light two candles and offer a prayer to Fulla. Then began laying out the objects that you have chosen to go into your treasure box. Quietly speak aloud what each object represents, why it is sacred to you, and why it deserves to be in your treasure box. When you are finished, think for a moment about those things that are missing from your box. Is there anything that you would like to add but felt that you could not? If asked, Fulla can help a person examine his or her life, looking deeply beneath the surface. Offer the box to Her now and ask Her aid. Ask Her to help you explore the hidden parts of yourself, the talents, wisdom, and strength that remains suppressed and secret. Spend as long as you want sitting in the presence of this Goddess, and when you are ready, thank Her, blow out the candles, and declare the rite over.

Saga

I hail Saga, Mistress of Sokkvabek,
Historian, Scop, Keeper of memory,
Collector of stories, preserver of truths,
Patroness of poets, sharp-tongued skald.
I will praise you with horn of mead,
with pen to page, with mindful thoughts
of connections and consequence and blood-red threads.
I will think upon You when I hail my dead, when I raise
    them to life with tales of their deeds.
I will hold You in my heart when I craft by action the
    story of my own life.
I will ask that You remember, when no others do,
those moments of quiet epiphanies which ask no
    celebration,
those moments of awareness so often unremarked by
    Your younger kin.
Let not my words pass into the void, You whose words
    are cunning and wise.

Give them power, that they may adhere to the fabric
of my wyrd as ink to the pristine page.
Let them stand with the weight of stone.
I hail Saga, Companion of Odin;
I hail Saga, ever-wise.

Saga's name comes from the Old Norse word *segja*, "to speak or to tell," and is related to the word for an epic tale. She is the historian of the Æsir, the collector of ancestral tales (perhaps one may infer from this that She is the genealogist of the Gods), the poet, skald, and memory keeper. Saga resides in a great hall named *Sokkvabekk* ("treasure bank" or "sunken bank") and is the frequent drinking companion of Odin.

In my own experiences with Saga, I have known Her as a Goddess who sets the patterns of one's life in order. She is an excellent Goddess for researchers, librarians, historians, and story-tellers to call upon. I personally have connected to Her most strongly as a writer, particularly when it comes to bringing old tales to light. As a skald, or a poet, Saga wields immense power. Skalds were held in very high esteem in Germanic culture, their skill with words being likened to a powerful type of magic. Personally, I have always found Saga very forthright and willing to speak Her mind, but also very genial. Because She is a historian, there is a strong ancestral element to Her work and a good way to honor Her may be to begin the ongoing project of researching and recording one's genealogy. Certainly She may be of aid in learning to honor one's Ancestors properly. Keeping a daily journal makes a lovely meditation activity for Her as well.

Eir

I will hail Eir, the Divine Physician.
Fortunate are those commended to Her care.
She is wise and mighty, and the weal of Her hands
strengthens the wounded.
Her works are filled with a ruthless compassion,
and to all things She brings the gift of fierce
contemplation.

I will praise this Mighty Goddess,
Whose touch upon our beings is like the fingers
of a master gardener
closing around a tiny seed and plunging it into
the rich, waiting earth.

Eir is renowned for Her healing abilities. She is mentioned in the surviving Eddic lore only twice, as the "best of physicians."[24] It is said that She provides healing to all women who seek Her out,[25] making them hale and whole again. Her name, Eir,[26] defines Her nature, translating from the Old Norse as "help" or "mercy."[27] She is also listed amongst the Valkyries, which connects Her to their power to awaken the dead, select the slain, and cut the threads of life.[28] Little else is known definitively about Her, but modern devotees of this Goddess know that Her healing is a gift She bestows on all levels: mental, emotional, physical, and most importantly of all, spiritual.

All healing herbs and tools are Hers, from the mortar and pestle to the Laece's[29] knife. She is Shaman as much as healer in that She restores both body and spirit to wholeness. Anglo-Saxon lore is rich with herbal charms and remedies designed to purge illness and negativity. Perhaps the most famous of these is "Wid Faerstice,"[30] a charm in which the healer commands the pain of elfshot[31] to leave the patient's body. While Eir is not mentioned specifically in this charm, it and the surviving Lacnunga manuscript[32] do provide evidence of an extremely well-developed system of healing in the Pre-Christian Heathen world. In fact, the experienced Heathen healer had a plethora of tools at his or her disposal: herbal remedies, surgical techniques, sauna, a form of acupuncture,[33] magico-religious charms, and the power of the runes to dispel harm and bind malignant forces, including disease. The healer, like the traditional Shaman, was then responsible for maintaining health (that is, wholeness) within his or her community.

Above all else, Eir is practical. There is no room for fluff or feel-good platitudes in this formidable Goddess. She is compassionate, but it is the detached, almost cold compassion of utter objectivity. There is a serenity about Her, a calm restraint that soothes, centers, and grounds.

In addition to being a Goddess of Healing, She may also be considered a Goddess of psycho-spiritual and physical harmony. Many who work with Her believe that She is, first and foremost, a Goddess of natural, alternative, and non-invasive healing techniques. Often Her folk will be found in the ranks of Reiki practitioners, feng shui practitioners, acupuncturists, massage therapists, naturopaths, herbalists, reflexologists, and the like. That does not mean that more invasive (surgical) techniques don't also fall under Her domain; they do. She is a surgeon as well as an herbal and magical healer. It is simply that She, more so than physicians in our modern era, embodies the dictum "First, do no harm."

Eir is a good Goddess to call upon when facing the proverbial "dark night of the soul." She can provide a calm lifeline through the spiritual descent, and we all know how such a process can highlight our hurt, broken places. Eir provides hope coupled with efficient, practical advice—provided we are willing to work hard and diligently at the areas She reveals. Eir is all about maintaining that emotional, psychic, and spiritual balance. Eir counsels us to walk a path of discipline, mindfulness, and moderation.

Meditation and Pathworking for Eir

Begin by setting up a simple altar to Eir. The altar should be simple, even stark. Set out a mortar and pestle, a knife, a chalice of fresh water, and any other symbols that you personally associate with Eir.

Begin by hallowing the space.

Prayer

I call upon You Eir, for help and inspiration.
I wish to be centered in You, sure in my purpose.
Assist me, Great Healer, in walking in mindfulness and kindness.
Do not let me wound by inadvertent word or deed;
Rather allow me to see clearly the right course of action.
Flow through me, bringing wholeness, health, and understanding.

Cleanse me of those things that would keep me
from being effective or whole.
Where I am weak, I know You will be strong.
Where I am afraid, I know that I shall have Your
guidance.
Hear me, mighty Eir, and know that my heart is
Your vessel.
Hail Healer of the Gods.

Take the chalice of water and offer it to Eir: "I offer You this water as a symbol of Your cleansing might. I ask for insight." Take a sip of the water and place the chalice back on the altar.

Meditation

Sit before the altar with your eyes closed and begin to focus on your breath. With each exhalation, feel the stress and tension of the mundane world falling away. Exhale it all; let it flow from you with the force of a rushing tide. Consciously release every bit of tension in your body, starting at the feet and slowly but surely working your way up to the crown of your head. Continue this until you are completely relaxed.

In your mind's eye, visualize yourself at the bottom of a green, lush mountain. Herbs and flowers, trees and foliage abound, and it is a place of calm serenity. There is a small dirt path leading up the mountain. Begin to follow it. There is no need to hurry. Take your time. Healing is a journey and so is this. Pay special attention to anything you may see as you walk, be it a unique animal, a special stone, or even a particular plant. Perhaps you will meet a fellow traveler on your journey. Perhaps you will gain some insight into what needs to be done in your upcoming healing session. Perhaps you will simply have a peaceful walk up a quiet hill.

At the top of the mountain, not immediately visible from the ground below, you find a small sanctuary. Taking a moment to still yourself, you enter. Inside, it is well lit, with sunlight streaming in from high open windows, and in the center of the main room, a fountain bubbles above a small cistern. Perhaps there are other healers moving to and fro, going about their work; perhaps it is silent, and you are the only visitor. Either way, it is obviously a place of healing. There are altars and herbs, sacred statues, and desperate petitions. Within the center of this healing place is a vast pool and fountain. The water bubbles invitingly. Meditate for a moment on water and its nature. It cleanses, restores, rejuvenates. It flows, seeping into every nook and cranny, finding its way into every crack, no matter how small. It can take the shape of whatever vessel it is contained within, yet never loses its essential nature. Healing is like that. It cannot be forced, only released and gently molded.

Go to the fountain and sit or kneel before it. Spend a few moments gazing into the water and note well any images or insights gained. If anyone approaches, listen well to their council. Perhaps it is Eir Herself or a worthy ancestress.[34] When you feel it is right, cup your hands and scoop up a handful of the healing water. It is filled with the vital energy of Eir Herself and of Her handmaidens.[35] Wash yourself with it, pouring the water over head and heart and hands. Take a second handful and bring it to your lips, imbibing a draught from the sacred spring. Then reach into your pocket and remove an object. Even you do not know what it will be. Place it on the rim of the cistern. This is the physical manifestation of those things that would interfere with your healing, preventing you from becoming as strong and whole as possible. Reach into the bubbling water in the cistern. Reach deep down to the bottom and draw forth a second object. This is what you need for your own insight or healing. Tuck it carefully away. It may be something that will help you bring healing to another, or it may be something that will help you personally in your own spiritual journey—only you will know at the time.

Spend as long as you need sitting before the fountain or exploring the healing temple. When you are ready, offer thanks to Eir and begin your descent down the mountain. As you descend, following the well-worn dirt path that first led you to the temple, each step brings you out of your journey, closer to temporal consciousness. As you walk, begin to focus again on your breath, slowly returning to yourself with each exhalation. Take a few moments at the end of your journey to ground, focusing on sending the excess energy in your body down into the earth like the roots of a strong, supple tree. When you are ready, open your eyes.

Gefion

Giving One, I ask Your blessings
on my mind and heart and life.
I would know You, Mighty Goddess,
beyond what remains of Your sacred tales.
Make me bold, as You are bold.
Make me mighty in spirit,
as You are mighty in all things.
I hail You, Gefion,
Goddess of plenty and might.

Gefion is mentioned in both Eddas and the Ynglings saga and is best known for the tale of how She won the island of Zealand from the Swedish King Gylfi. She appeared to him as a vagrant, and as a reward for some unspoken entertainment She had given him, he told Her that he would give her as much land as She was able to plow around in a single day and night. What King Gylfi didn't know is that the vagrant woman was in fact a Goddess of the Æsir. She hurried off to Jotunheim, married a giant, and birthed four strong sons whom She transformed into oxen. She returned to Gylfi's realm and, using Her four sons to pull the plough, ploughed so hard and fast that the entire island of Zealand was ploughed loose from the mainland. She is remembered to this day and there is even a fountain in Copenhagen that depicts Gefion with Her plough.

Gefion's name means "The Giving One," and many modern Heathens call upon Her for help with their finances, financial management, and investing. Given Her story, She may be hailed as a Goddess of wise acquisition, prosperity, and material wealth. She is a wise, far-seeing Goddess, and Odin chides Loki in the Lokasenna for harassing Her, noting that Gefion sees the fate of all men as clearly as He Himself does.

Gná

Swift Goddess Gná,
strong in purpose,
I hail You.

Divine Messenger,
with ease You traverse the Worlds.
I praise You as You guide Your steed
across Bifrost Bridge, never faltering, never hesitating,
always quick and sure.
No obstacle bars Your way.
No enemy is able to draw near.
I would be like You:
Sure of myself, sure in my purpose,
unyieldingly brave in my journey into the unknown.
Hail, Gná!

Gná is Frigga's messenger. She travels throughout the nine worlds, going about the Allmother's business. Her name comes from the Old Norse verb *gnæfa*, which means "to tower or rise high," for She rides high in the air on the back of Her steed, Hofvarpnir (Hoof-Thrower). Nothing else is known about Her through the lore, though it may be posited that She would be of excellent aid in overcoming obstacles and in moving forward in one's life. She may also be willing to aid in clear communication in all aspects of life. I would ask Her assistance in all problems that require a speedy resolution.

Syn

Guardian Goddess, protect me, I pray.
Let no threat breach the hall of my heart.
Protect me from the violence of others' tongues.
Protect me from the violence of their wills and words.
Let no weapon harm me. Guard the threshold of my person.
Make of me an impenetrable fortress to those who wish only ill.
I hail You, mighty Gatekeeper. I hail You, mighty Syn.

Syn is generally seen as a protective guardian Goddess, and the Eddas describe Her as the gatekeeper of Fensalir. She maintains the frith of the hall by barring the doors to those who would create disruption. Her name means "denial" or "refusal," and there is some evidence that She may have had a role on the side of the defense in legal assemblies. Simek connects Her to the Matronæ, Tribal Mother Goddesses to whom votary stones were erected by the Germanic tribes.[36]

Hlín

I call upon Your strength, Mighty Hlín.
Defend me, I pray, for on all sides I am beset by danger.
Still the fear that gnaws like a hungry worm at my heart;
Shield me, Oh Goddess.
Let nothing harm me, not fire nor water nor wind nor
evil intention.
Guard me and guide me, I pray.
Hail Mighty Hlín.

Hlín's name means "protectress," and She is specifically charged with protecting those mortals favored by Frigga. She is a refuge of those in grave danger. In my own experiences with Her, I have found that She is reserved and formidable, almost cold in demeanor and very watchful. She is weapons-wise and a deadly warrior. Those whom She chooses to defend are unassailable by any threat.

She may also be a Goddess to call upon when in the throes of heart-breaking grief. The Voluspa notes:

Another woe awaited Hlín,
when forth goes Óthin to fight the wolf
and the slayer of Beli to battle with Surt:
then Frigg's husband will fall lifeless."[37]

Some Heathens interpret this to mean that Hlín is but a byname of Frigga, but to others, She is a companion of Frigga who will provide the fortitude to continue after the death of Frigga's husband at Ragnarokk. Perhaps She was called upon by women who had lost their spouses in battle to help anneal the terrible grief and loneliness. Regardless, the

Eddas list Her as a Goddess in Her own right, and She has much to teach about personal pride, integrity, and assertive self-protection.

Sjöfn and Lofn

Gentle Goddesses, open my heart to love.
Let me not despair, but guide me through the tangles
of those relationships I cherish.
Let me not cause pain to another's heart,
but let not my own heart wither
in the face of love's challenges.
I hail You, for the comfort and hope You bring.
I hail You for smoothing the way not only in love
but in all human interactions.
Hail Sjöfn, Hail Lofn. I thank you.

Both of these Goddesses are concerned with love. Sjöfn's name is from the Old Norse word *siafni*, which means "affection," and She helps smooth the way for productive interaction between people, not just in the realm of love, but in all dealings. She opens the heart to appreciation of those relationships that nourish us. She opens the heart to love, be it romantic love or the love of a good friend.

Lofn's name means "Comforter," and it is She that gives hope when in the midst of difficult challenges in a relationship. The Eddas note that She was so kind-hearted that She would go out of Her way to procure permission from Frigga and Odin for couples to marry, even if they were previously forbidden to wed. She provides hope in the midst of relationship troubles and counsels patience and resolve. The word for "permission" (*lof*) is derived from Her name.[38]

Vor

Hail, Wise Goddess.
Nothing escapes Your sharp gaze.
You see into the deepest recesses of my heart.
You see everything, even that which I would hide
in shame.

May I be bettered in Your sight.
May all the secrets of my heart be revealed to You
with pride.
May I stand before You a man/woman of worth.
Hail, Vor.

Almost nothing is known about Vor, save that She was extremely perceptive. In the *Prose Edda*, it is noted that She is wise and careful and never misses anything. In my opinion, She may be hailed as a Goddess of self-discovery, self-exploration, and what psychologists call "shadow work." She would likewise be an excellent ally during the proverbial "dark night of the soul." She is a Goddess of all things unseen.

Var

I hail You, Var,
Guardian of all that is wise and just.
You set our souls gently yet firmly
on the path of truth and integrity.
I welcome You as a shining guide.
Let my words honor You.
Let my actions praise Your name.
May I always walk in truth, bound only by my sworn word.
I know it will be difficult.
Guide me through the fear.
May I always find shelter and guidance
beneath Your staff.
Illuminate my words, give life to the vows I make this day
that I never have cause to face You in shame.

Traditionally, Var is the Goddess who witnesses all sacred oaths, particularly marriage oaths. Her name means "vow" or "pledge," and the contracts made by oath between men and women are called *varar*. The Eddas point out that She punishes those who break their sworn word. The breaking of a sacred vow impacts the luck of all involved, including one's family and tribe. Such a thing was a grievous wrong in Germanic society. Var could then be said to maintain the strength and purity of the tribal Hamingja by punishing oath-breakers.

Meditation on Var

Hallow the space and offer up a prayer to Var. After calling to Her, sit down and engage in a brutally honest critique of the past year(s), addressing any problems and coming to workable solutions. The good should be discussed as well as the bad. What goals have you set for yourself? What promises have you made to yourself and others. Have you upheld them? Where have you fallen short? In what ways do you break your word? In what ways do you sacrifice the power of your speech by promising that which you cannot deliver? Think about this long and hard. Take as much time as necessary. Are you the kind of person you wish to be? Could you face Var at this very moment proudly, with no stain of broken oaths, broken promises, or hastily spoken words on your Hamingja?

Once you have completed your self-examination, take a glass of wine. Offer some challenging part of your life to Var for the coming year along with a promise to transform, confront, or resolve it. Offer two things: one for yourself personally and one for the good of your tribe or kin-group as a whole. Heat a needle in a flame until it is red hot, and prick your finger, offering a few drops of blood to Var by dripping it into the wine and promising to adhere to the preceding oath. Thank Var for Her patience and take the wine outside, pouring it out into the earth in offering to Her. Once the rite is finished, wash and clean your hands, bandaging your finger.

> **(Note: Please use common sense. With any type of cut or puncture, there is a risk of infection. Never, ever, share cutting implements with anyone. This is meant to be done as a solitary meditation. Be sure to use alcohol, bacitracin, or some other antiseptic to cleanse the puncture; even small wounds can become infected. It is perfectly okay not to do this part of the meditation; a simple vow can be spoken over the wine by itself.)**

Snotra

Gracious Goddess, clever and wise,
I hail You with horn upraised.
You are Goddess of right action,
of courtesy and personal integrity.
Yours is the steel hand in the velvet glove.
You know when to conceal Your power
and when it should be revealed.
I praise You, Snotra, I would learn from You
how best to navigate the most difficult situations.

Snotra is another Goddess in Frigga's retinue of whom very little is known. Her name means "clever" or "wise" and is derived from the Norse word *snotr*, meaning "a clever person." She is said to be a Goddess of proper behavior and courtesy. Some modern Heathens see Her as a Goddess akin to the Emily Post of the Æsir, but I personally see Her as the consummate diplomat—clever in Her speech, able to navigate the most challenging of social situations with aplomb and grace, and capable of great persuasion to Her cause, whatever it may be.

Baldur and Nanna

Brave Warrior, Shining Lord of Justice and Mercy,
 we ask for Your blessings and grace.
Compassion flows from Your strong heart
 and noble brow.
Fearless Lord of Death and rebirth, intrepid,
 You have braved the realm of Hel,
So that we, children of the Gods, might have a champion
 to greet us when we too make this perilous journey.
Warrior-born, fill our hearts with Thy quiet courage.
Do not let us falter on our life's journey.
Teach us serenity of spirit that we might face
 the turmoil of our lives
joyously, embracing destiny without fear.

Open our hearts and let us not shrink in terror
from our descent
into the earth, but find in Her dark depths
spiritual renewal.
May we live lives of courage, passion, and valor.
Hail, Baldur!

Gentle Nanna, Baldur's devoted wife,
extend over us Your blessings and protection,
for we often struggle in our lives feeling lost and alone.
Stand with us as You stood with Baldur, even joining
Him in Hel's realm.
Sustain us, nourish us, and grant us the gift
of Your compassion.
Hail Nanna, Daring and Bold, Compassionate One, Hail.

Baldur was the beloved son of Oðinn and Frigga, husband of the Goddess Nanna and, by some sources, father of Forseti. His death was foretold by a seeress consulted after He experienced a series of unsettling dreams. In order to protect Baldur from harm, Frigga traveled the worlds extracting an oath from every living thing that it will never harm Her son. She neglected to gain such an oath from mistletoe, however, thinking it too insignificant to do any harm. Sure that He was safe from His foretold fate, the Gods celebrated and boldly made a game of tossing weapons and darts at Baldur. Each missile bounced off harmlessly. Loki, however, made a dart out of mistletoe and gave it to Baldur's brother, the blind God Hoðr. With Loki guiding His hand, Hoðr tossed the dart, and it killed Baldur instantly. Baldur was placed on a funeral ship, and Oðinn whispered final words to His son, placing His holy ring Draupnir in Baldur's dead hands. Nanna died of grief upon seeing the funeral barge and was placed beside Her husband. The ship was set on fire, as was Germanic custom at the time, and so Baldur journeyed to Hel, the land of the all the dead who do not die in battle or in service to a specific God. Hoðr was slain by His half brother Vali, in vengeance for His crime.

Oðinn and Frigga were so distraut by His death that They sent Their other son, Hermod, to Hel, to ask Her to release Baldur and Nanna. She agreed to do this if every living thing would weep for the dead God. All did, save one: Loki took the form of an old woman and refused to weep, saying that Hel should keep what She has. (Given that Hel is Loki's daughter, it is none too surprising to find that He would not wish to rob Her of the wealth of Her realm.) Baldur and Nanna, therefore, have to remain in the land of the dead and, by doing so, survive Ragnarokk.

Nanna is Baldur's wife and very little is known of Her, save that, by some accounts, Her name may translate as "the Daring One."[39] According to author Saxo Grammaticus, Nanna is married not to Baldur, but to His brother, Hoðr. Both Hoðr and Baldur survive Ragnarokk.

Forseti

I hail Forseti, wise in His judgements.
I praise His far-seeing wisdom.
He sets the law and orders the Thing.
He watches over His folk and protects them.
I hail this Shining God. I will praise Him often,
with raised horn and right deeds.

In the Eddas, Forseti is said to be the son of Baldur and Nanna and master of the Hall Glitnir ("Glittering") within Asgard. It is highly likely, however, that He is a much older God as He is referenced in eighth-century English sources as a Frisian God of law. When Charlemagne demanded the Frisians produce a law code, the elders of the tribe managed to delay fulfilling this request twice, but finally were punished by being sent out in a rudderless boat. They petitioned their God, and a radiant man appeared bearing a golden ax. He guided the boat ashore on an uninhabited island and threw His ax into the earth where a spring appeared. Then He began to speak, giving the Frisian elders their law code. The sacred spring was later desecrated by a Christian missionary who very nearly lost his life for the affront.

Today, Forseti is honored as overseer of the Thing assembly, as well as a God of law, judges, and just ruling. Specifically, He is one who actually creates and sets laws, giving them to His people. Personally, I see Him clothed in white linen and find edelweiss to be a welcome offering.

Heimdall (Hama)

Hail Heimdall, Shining Watcher of Asgard.
Hail, the strength of the Æsir.
Hail to Your never-tiring vigilance;
With You on the bridge, man and Gods rest secure.
I hail Your fortitude, never resting, never sleeping.
You, too, sacrificed at the well of Mimir.
I hail Your commitment to Your duty,
Purest of the Gods, Holy watchman on the Bridge.
Your presence alone banishes fear and threat.
You maintain the integrity of the inangarð.
Your mindfulness is a gift to us all.
I hail You, Valiant One!

Heimdall is the watchman of the Gods. He stands on Bifrost bridge with a gleaming horn, which will be blown to alert the Gods when any threat approaches. He is the son of nine mothers, daughters of Aegir and Ran, and His name means "One who illuminates the world."[40] By some accounts, it was Heimdall who wandered the earth under the name Rig, siring children on each couple that offered Him hospitality, thus becoming Father of mankind. Some scholars believe Rig to have been Oðinn (and certainly this fits His modus operandi), but others point to the Voluspa, where mankind is referred to as "Heimdall's children."[41]

Heimdall has a number of heiti that point to His importance in Eddic cosmology. He is called Hallinskísði ("Ram"), Gullintani ("Gold-toothed"), Vindler ("Protector Against the Wind" or possibly "Wind-Sea"), and Whitest of the Ás. He has a hall in Asgard called Himinbjorg ("Heavenly Mountain"), and it is said that He sacrificed an ear to the well of Mimir in order to gain exceptional hearing. Indeed, Heimdall is a God possessed of many exceptional abilities befitting a sentry and guardsman. His hearing is so acute that He can hear the grass growing on Midgard. He needs less sleep than a bird, and His vision is as keen as His hearing regardless of whether it be day or night. He also possesses the ability to change His shape at will. When Loki attempted to steal Freya's magical necklace (and symbol of Her power) Brisingamen, Heimdall spied Him as He fled and set off in pursuit. Eventually Heimdall caught up with Loki near the ocean, and the two Gods transformed into seals, battling for possession of the necklace in animal form. Heimdall won the battle, and the necklace was returned to Freya. Because of this, Heimdall and Loki are deadly enemies, and it is said that each will be the destruction of the other at Ragnarokk.[42]

Heimdall is a God of keen, mindful vigilance, and because of that, some Heathens today honor Him as a God of spiritual growth and contemplation.[43]

Ullr (Wuldor)

Cold, You are called, and harsh.
God of barren, forgotten places—
remote, unapproachable, fierce as wolf on the hunt.
But I have not found You thus.
I have felt Your gift of quiet strength and comfort many times.
I think that You are God of all forgotten creatures,
those neglected souls bereft of love.
You teach us to sing a song of power and beauty
in the lonely wasteland of our scarred and broken hearts.
You are Father to all those children called ugly, ignorant, or wrong.
All little creatures in need of love are welcome in Your hall.
No pain is too great for You to succor, no agony too great for You to bear.
Do You weep, in the solitude of Your ice-scaped dwelling,
as You seek those lost and bleeding souls, their number sadly beyond measure?

No one thinks to go to You for healing, yet that is the gift You bring,
God of all orphaned hearts.
All who hear the song of the ice-blessed darkness may count themselves blessed by its sweetness.
I hail You, Son of Sif, Mighty Ullr, Glorious God.

Ullr is another of those Gods of which very little established lore has survived. We know that He is the son of Sif, but we do not know who His father is, save that it *isn't* Thor. His name means "glory" and He lives in a realm called Ýdalir, or "Yew-Dales." He is renown as a great archer, skier, and hunter and was often invoked for aid in single combat. He was a God of the lone warrior and a common kenning for shield was "Ullr's ship." Numerous place names, most of them with suffixes[44] indicating that they were considered holy places, are connected to Him, indicating that He was likely very highly honored at one time. Some sources go so far as to say that Ullr ruled Asgard in Oðinn's absence. There is some indication that Ullr was a good God to call upon in making oaths. Today, Ullr is primarily honored as a God of hunting, and many of His heiti attest to His skill: Bogaáss ("Bow God"), Veiðáss ("Hunting God"), and Ønduráss ("Ski God").

Hoenir (Hana) and Loður

Odin's brother, holy Prophet, Shining Ás,
I raise this horn to You.
Hostage to the Vanir, Ancient Creator, Frith-weaver,
I honor Your quiet courage.
Bestower of spirit and conscious awareness,
God of mindful contemplation,
I praise You for these mighty gifts.
I have found You unassuming in Your wisdom.
I have learned to cherish simplicity from Your graceful example.
I hail You Hoenir, with this horn and in my heart.
I hail You with reverence.

Hail, Loður, God of passion and warmth.
Because of Your gift, we are able to experience the world.
Because of Your gift, we are able to know pleasure through our five senses.
You are the beating of our hearts, the rhythm of our blood.
You have given life to our bodies as breath; sense and will were given by Your brothers.
I hail You, Divine enigma, known to us only as Odin's friend.
God of beauty, You inspire growth. From You we are given our evolutionary drive.
I hail You, for Your gifts at the time the world was born. Hail, Loður.

Hoenir is the brother of Oðin, who with Him helped to create the first man and woman by bestowing the gifts of consciousness and will. Hoenir was given as hostage to the Vanir to ensure peace after the first war, and sources credit Him with maintaining that peace even after the slaying of Mimir. Hoenir is slow of speech but considered very wise, perhaps embodying the Norse ideal, exemplified in the "Havamal," of wisdom going hand in hand with silence.[45] He occasionally traveled with the Gods and is generally described as tall and handsome. He apparently had a very close relationship with Mimir, who was very likely His maternal uncle. Many modern Heathens hail Him as a God of prophecy and vision. Hoenir is one of the Gods said to survive Ragnarokk.

Even less is known about Loður. Some attempts have been made to link Him to Loki, but without definitive success. During the creation of humanity, Loður gave the gifts of the five senses and beauty of form. He gave rhythm to beating of the heart and the pulse of the blood, the essence of life and being. Nothing more is known of Him and it remains for modern Heathens to rediscover His worship.

Hermod

I hail You, Hermod, for Your bravery.
Hermod, I want to be like You.

I do not wish to fear the dark places within my soul
or to shy away from understanding.
You went riding into Hel
to save Your brother;
did You know then that You were saving Yourself as well?
You are God of unexpected catalysts,
of journeys and the battle we fight within.
I, too, would mount the spirit steed
that would carry me to the places
of power and change.
Will You ride with me, Hermod?
Will You protect me from myself
As I ride the path to heaven?
The loneliness held no terror for You,
Teach me, silent One, to be staunch in my journey.
Let my heart not be turned from this path,
by the vagaries and fears of my own spirit.
Let me journey, as You did so long ago,
firm and bold, as I hold my hand unwavering
up to heaven.

Hermod is the son of Oðinn, brother of the God Baldur. After Baldur's death, Hermod was sent to Hela's realm to bargain for His brother's release, having borrowed Oðinn's eight-legged steed, Sleipnir, for the journey. His journey took nine long nights, during which He faced the giantess Moðguðr, Guardian of the gates of Hel. She initially challenged Him but, upon learning the reason for His journey, granted Him passage into the land of the dead. Once inside Helheim, Hermod was granted access to Baldur and Nanna, who had been given places of honor within Hel's hall. He attempted to negotiate with Hela for Baldur's return, and She agreed on the condition that every living thing weep for the fallen God. (All living things did, save one: an old woman, Þokk, who was really Loki in disguise.) Before Hermod returned to the realm of the Gods, Baldur asked Him to return Oðinn's armring, Draupnir, which His father had placed on the funeral ship with Him, and Nanna sends gifts back to

Frigga. Hermod is the only God known to have been granted access into the land of the dead while in living form. Even Oðinn never actually entered Hela's gates.

Njorðr

I hail Njorðr, God of wealth and plenty.
I celebrate the treasures He brings forth from the sea.
I praise His tranquil nature, He who was sent as
peace-weaver
to the Æsir. I hail His ability to reach compromise
in the most heated of situations.
He is wise and far-seeing, gentle and open-handed.
I hail the Master of Noatun, Husband of Skadhi,
Father of Freyr and Freya.
Smile upon us in our endeavors, and in all things
make our hearts fruitful, Oh Lord.
To You, God of fair trade and exploration, of right gain
and fruitful bounty, I pray.

Njordr is the father of Frey and Freya, and he was one of the Gods sent to the Æsir as a hostage for peace at the end of the war between the Æsir and the Vanir. As such, He is a Vanic God and, like many of the Vanir, is intimately connected to the bounty and fertility of the land. In the case of Njordr, His realm is Noatun, the Ship-yard, and He governs wealth that is won from the sea. He is specifically considered to be a God of fair commerce and trade. Njordr is sometimes linked with the Goddess Nerthus as brother-lover, and Their names correspond etymologically. Njordr was often called upon to aid both sailors and fisherman for protection, as well as for luck and prosperity. Though very little is actually known about Njordr from surviving sources, given the importance of seafaring to the Germanic culture—particularly the Vikings—His influence should not be quickly dismissed.

The most well-known story involving Njordr is that of His marriage to the Jotun warrior Skaði. Once, Loki was captured by Thjazi, Skaði's father. Thjazi would only agree to free Loki if Loki would promise to bring him the Goddess Iðunn, with Her apples of immortality and youth, in return. Having no choice, for Thjazi had Loki well and truly trapped, Loki agreed. He was freed and returned to Asgard where, at first opportunity, He lured Iðunn out by tricking Her into thinking He had found an apple tree with apples just like Hers. Her curiosity was Her undoing. Once She was in Thjazi's clutches, Loki turned the tables and, upon facing the Gods' collective wrath, promised to secure Her return. He did so, but Thjazi was killed in the process. As a consequence, Skaði armed Herself and stormed Asgard demanding retribution and wergild.[46] The Gods agreed but had to meet Skaði's conditions. She wasn't, after all, going to make it easy for Them. Odin tossed Her father's eyes into the sky where they would gleam for all eternity as stars. Additionally, She was to be allowed to choose a husband from the assembled Gods, and finally, She had to be made to laugh. As She had just lost Her father, this might have proven a difficult task had Loki not saved the day. He cavorted about and finally tied his testicles to the beard of a goat. The goat took off in fright, causing Loki to tumble in an ungainly fashion into Skaði's lap. The sight was so bizarre that She laughed out loud. Next, all the Gods assembled, and Skaði was allowed to choose Her mate. There was a catch though: She had to choose Them by Their feet only. Skaði had Her eye set on Baldr and chose what She considered to be the most beautiful feet there, thinking that surely, as the most beautiful of Gods, Baldr would have beautiful feet. Instead of Baldr, however, She chose Njordr, whose feet were beautiful from having been washed repeatedly in the ocean waves, for He often walked along the beaches of His seaside dwelling. Again playing the peace-maker, Njordr married Skaði, and She became a shining Bride of the Gods. The marriage however, was not a success. The couple tried to compromise on Their living situation, spending nine days in Noatun and nine days in Skaði's home, Thrymheim, but She could not stand the relentless squawking of the gulls, and He could not tolerate the howling of the wolves and wind. Eventually, They parted amicably.

Perhaps Njordr could also be hailed as a God of negotiations and diplomacy. I have known many Heathens who chose to call upon Him for aid in navigating the corporate world, precisely to gain the benefit of His calm counsel and ability to find a workable compromise to any situation.

Skaði (Sceadu)

I raise this horn to the etin bride of winter.
I praise Skaði, fierce warrior, Defender of Her father.
She is bold, fierce, and vicious in Her cunning.
She is passionate, focused, a steadfast ally.
Bride of Njord, Lover of Woden, fettered by none,
I will seek You, Skaði, in places of solitude.
I will seek You in the icy cold of winter.
The freezing wind is Your breath, the pristine snow
Your mantle.
Formidable huntress, I will be Your willing prey.
Seek me out. I will not flee.
Come into my dark places, and we will celebrate
them together.
I hail You, Skaði. I offer this to You.

I have always had a particular affinity for Skaði. She is formidable, unyielding, and fierce. Her willingness to seek vengeance with blade and shield if need be, speak of Her pride in Her heritage and Her skills as warrior, for She was willing to take on all of Asgard *by Herself.* She bows Her head to no one and can be quite vicious in protecting Her domain. She does not compromise Herself for anyone or anything, and those are virtues I quite admire. Additionally, as a woman involved in the martial arts, Skaði has been an inspiration to me—a Goddess that I have often called upon for fortitude in my training.

Skaði's name means "shadow," and She is associated with the barren, winter landscape; wolves; skiing; bow-hunting; and physical fitness. Modern Heathens hail Her as a huntress and Goddess of winter and as one of the etin brides (Jotun women who married into the Æsir or Vanir and were thus elevated to Godhood). She is the cousin of the etin bride Gerða, and when Njordr's son Freyr fell ill with love-sickness after having seen Gerða from afar, it was Skaði who first noticed His malady. Many places in Scandinavia are named after Her, though there is very little about Her in lore. She is called "Shining Bride of the Gods," and Öndurdís ("Dis of the Snow Shoe"). At some point, She and Oðinn were lovers, and She had at least one son by Him, from which a royal line in Norway is descended.[47] Some modern Heathens attempt to link Skaði and Ullr as a Divine couple, though there is nothing to support this in lore.

Skaði is responsible for the binding of Loki after the death of Baldr. After it is discovered (by His own words, no less) that Loki was responsible for guiding Hoðr's hand, the Gods chase Him down and capture Him, though He tries to flee by changing shape into that of a salmon. He is taken to a dank cave deep in the earth and tethered to a rock with the entrails of His own son. Skaði takes a poisonous serpent and secures it above Him so that the venom will drip onto His face. Loki's wife, Sigyn, remains by His side, doing Her best to capture the venom in a bowl. It can only be assumed that Skaði's eventual enmity toward Loki hearkens back to His role in the death of Her father. She is not one to forgive such things easily.

Skaði continues to be highly honored today and provides a particularly good role model for women who, either in personal or professional life, choose not to follow society's accepted norm.

Nerthus

Holy Nerthus, Terra Mater, I hail You.
You guard Your secrets wisely and well,
and to You, we owe our sustenance.
In dawnlight and in darkness I praise You,
Mother of the damp, dark earth.
I celebrate Your bounty with words and proffered wine.
I celebrate You with action and mindful contemplation of the earth and Her resources.
I remember, Goddess, Tribal Mother, that once Your sacred cart
circumnavigated the land as offerings were given to Your image.

I hold You in awe, Goddess. I hail You with
deepest respect.
Hail, Mighty Nerthus.

The Goddess Nerthus is known only from Tacitus's *Germania*. She was an earth Goddess revered by several Baltic and Germanic tribes, including the Angles who later settled England. Tacitus records a rite in which a cart bearing the veiled image of this Goddess was led by Her priest throughout the tribal lands. No one was permitted to view the holy image except for the priest:

> On an island of the sea stands an inviolate grove, in which, veiled with a cloth, is a chariot that none but the priest may touch. The priest can feel the presence of the goddess in this holy of holies, and attends her with deepest reverence as her chariot is drawn along by cows. Then follow days of rejoicing and merrymaking in every place that she condescends to visit and sojourn in. No one goes to war, no one takes up arms; every iron object is locked away. Then, and then only, are peace and quiet known and welcomed until the goddess, when she has had enough of the society of men, is restored to her sacred precinct by the priest. After that, the chariot, the vestments, and (believe it if you will) the goddess herself, are cleansed in a secluded lake. This service is performed by slaves who are immediately after drowned in the lake. Thus mystery begets terror and a pious reluctance to ask what that sight can be which is only seen by men doomed to die."[48]

Tacitus compared Nerthus to the Roman Terra Mater. Examining how the Romans viewed their Earth Mother may provide useful clues to the nature of Nerthus. The Romans were well aware not only of the nourishing gifts of the Earth, but of Her terrible power as well: earthquakes, famine, flood, storm, and destruction. She was beautiful and life-giving, terrifying and destructive all at once. There was bounty, but also immense danger contained in the holy presence of this Goddess, and so it was with Nerthus as well, as the previous passage from Tacitus attests.

Frey (Fro Ing/Ingvi Freyr/Freá)

I hail Freyr, God of the earth,
Bringer of bounty to all barren places.
I hail Your sweetness of heart, Your passion,
Your strength.
I hail Your life-giving hands and Your gentleness.
God of rain, gentle breezes, and fertile fields,
I ask Your blessing on my heart, mind, and spirit.
I ask that You bring peace and abundance to my life,
and with my creativity, I will honor You.
Hail, Freyr.

Freyr is one of the most beloved of Heathen Gods today. His name means "lord" in Old Norse, and He is indeed Lord of fertility, sexual union, abundance, prosperity, ancestral might, and harvest. He brings blessings and fertility to crops, livestock, creative endeavors, and individuals wishing children, and luck to the community at large. Freyr is a God of Kingship, and as such, His blessings make the land fruitful and prosperous. Conversely, He also plays a role in war, and the boar is His symbol, both as an emblem of fertility and also as a symbol of strength in battle. Freyr owned a golden boar named Gullinbursti ("Golden Bristled"), and in sacred rituals, holy oaths were often sworn by placing one's hand on the sacrificial pig. Furthermore, a certain type of berserker warrior drew the inspiration for their battle frenzy not from the bear or wolf, as was most common, but from the boar. The image of the boar often appeared on helmets and weaponry, to imbue the strength of the sacred animal on the warrior. Freyr is the only God who fights without a weapon at Ragnarokk, having sacrificed His sword to win His bride Gerða.

Because He is said to have fathered a line of Kings, Freyr is a tribal God, and the royal line of Sweden traces its ancestry back to Him. There is some evidence that Freyr's priests cross-dressed in pre-Christian times, and there are references to bells being worn by the priests and dances being performed in His honor, though this may simply be a reference to the Vanic taboo of wearing belts or knots during rites, which would result in robes flowing loosely. Some modern Heathens even believe that Morris dancing evolved from rites performed in honor of Freyr. His heiti are numerous: Árguð ("Harvest God"), Bjartr ("Bright"), Bödfróðr ("Battle Wise"), Díar ("Priest"), Fégjafa ("Wealth-giver"), Máttug ("Mighty"), Nýtum ("Providing"), and Fólkvaldi goða ("Ruler of the People"), to name but a few.

Freyr is also a God of sensual pleasure. The most well-known story of Freyr is that of His courtship with the Jotun maiden Gerða. In Asgard, Oðinn had a high seat named Valaskjalf from which He could see everything that passed far and wide in any of the worlds. No one was permitted to sit in Valaskjalf but the Allfather. One day while Oðinn was wandering the earth on one of His many journeys, Freyr snuck into Gladsheim and sat in Oðinn's chair. Looking out across all the worlds His attention was drawn to Jotunheim, where He saw a lovely maiden for the briefest of moments. Those few moments were enough however to kindle in Him an intense love and desire. He pined for days, unable to eat or sleep, until His stepmother Skaði sent Freyr's faithful friend and servant Skirnir to find out what was wrong.

Skirnir finally coerced the source of the sickness and anguish out of his master and, at Freyr's pleading, agreed to journey to Jotunheim to woo Gerða for Him (as was the custom of the Germanic tribes). In return, He asked for Freyr's sword, which will fight by itself, and also His horse. Freyr surrendered both horse and sword willingly, and Skirnir set off. He was granted access to Gerða's hall, but the Jotun woman was not overly keen to accept Freyr's proposal and repeatedly refused. Skirnir grew frustrated and resorted to questionable methods to win her acquiescence: He first threatened violence, which Gerða proudly dismissed. Eventually, Skirnir cursed her with three powerful runes, using thurisaz, the most destructive and dangerous rune in the entire futhark. The runes would have compelled an unquenchable lust, and Ann Groa Sheffield, in her work "Frey: God of the World," speculates that the "magic of the runes and potions represents Frey's power to awaken sexual desire."[49] Regardless, Gerða agreed to meet Freyr in a sacred grove nine nights hence and thereby accepted His suit.

It is telling that, in the "Lokasenna," Freyr is referred to as one who has never made any girl or man's wife cry; in other words, He has never mistreated a woman. He is a God of vitality and life force so abundant that it cannot possibly be contained. Much of His iconography pictures Him with a large, erect phallus for just this reason. He brings life in all its manifold forms, and He blesses loving unions in all their many forms as well. He is a God not only of sensual pleasure, but of joy and happiness, bestowing those gifts freely upon His folk.

Gerða (Gearde)

I hail Gerda, shining bride of Frey.
I honor Her for Her self-possession, Her independence,
Her ferocity of spirit.
She is primal power, like a river rushing beneath the ice.
She is raw force, incantations whispered in the darkness,
the embodiment of Ginungagap's synergy.
She is silent contemplation, the holder of all things secret.
She is the loss that is not seen, the holder of life that is
not born.
I hail Gerda, for all that She has taught me.
I hail Her for being the shadow that illuminates and
nourishes Frey.

Very little is known about Gerða, save that She is the bride of Freyr, cousin of Skaði, and that Her name means "enclosure." She is the daughter of the giants Gymir and Aurboða and is listed amongst the Asynjur. Many scholars generally interpret the marriage of Gerða and Freyr as a sacred marriage: the barren, wintry earth melting and bearing life when touched by the sun, but this is, perhaps, overly simplistic. Simek points out that the etymology of Her name relates not to the actual enclosed land, but to the actual act of fencing it off.[50] While She may indeed represent the barren earth seduced into new life, there is much more to Her than that. She has a certain implacable quality that is reserved, contained, and secret. It gives itself sparingly and only to those it finds worthy. Gerða is one who finds the sacred within Herself. And that, I think, is the meaning behind the translation of her name as "enclosure." She has found within herself the most sacred of temples and will not willingly open those doors to just anyone. Gerða preserves the self.

It is a very important gift she gives, that preservation of the self. We are the greatest gifts we can give our Gods, and that cannot be done unless we know truly who we are and what our foundation is. Trance work, spiritual work, pathworkings, journey work—all of this can be dangerous for the unknowing soul, which then learns only to bend to whatever wind blows the strongest. Gerða prevents that. She is staunch within herself; She guards herself and challenges the interloper. That is what I personally believe lies behind the secret of her courtship with Frey. She does not suffer well the spiritually complaisant. She tests, as all wisdom must test. It is Gerða who treasures those thorny places within the heart. She keeps the heart from falseness. She gives only to those she has found worthy. She does not offer of herself to please or to be liked. She watches all, observes all, and chooses very carefully where to share of Her energy. That is not something many women can say. She is content within herself.

To return again to the meaning of Her name, "enclosure" is the sacred space, the *vé* (the Norse word for "altar") upon which all offerings are made. It is a place of devotion, a place to be protected and treasured. That she is a giantess indicates that She has the potential to manifest the forces of chaos and destruction—awesome, primal power. Yet She controls them, encloses them in strictest self-mastery. She treasures Her immense passion but is not ruled by it. She puts things in their place. Hers is the inward manifestation of Skaði's outward mastery.

My own experience with Gerða has taught me that She cares about bonds, about upholding them and maintaining them. She teaches us to honor our ancestors; to listen to their voices and to find wisdom in stones, trees, and wind. There is an unspoken balance and icy clarity about Her presence. She teaches how to maintain the integrity of our bonds, to strengthen our Hamingja, and to pass on that strength. She teaches us to honor and connect past to present and to strive for future goals while nurturing our present.

I see Her very much as a solitary Goddess, for all that She is associated with Freyr. They are in many ways beautifully complimentary. They accept and cherish each other's differences. She is a Goddess of all loss that is not seen. I have called upon Her when counseling women who had recently miscarried. She is the shadow to Freyr's light, and as He brings life, She honors life that does not come to fruition. Gerða is self-contained, and that is the lesson that She will gladly teach to those who come to Her. She teaches self-respect. Her children do not barter themselves for a moment's pleasure or comfort. They are unswerving, unyielding, and maintain the sacred enclosure of their souls. She teaches us how to bear hurt rather than yield to that which is not true. She teaches us to wait, to be content in the silence of our spirits, to seek out that silent, centered place, and from there, blossom.

Freya (Fréo)

I will hail the Goddess of gold,
Hostage to the Gods, delight of Her kin.
I will praise Her with amber and wine,
flowers and honey, for She is Goddess of beauty,
eroticism, and desire.
I will celebrate Her abundance, Her gifts of wealth
and fruitful plenty.
She brings luck, fertility, and creative fire, and Her
presence is found
amid the moaning cry of lovers, hidden within the
rhythm of their entwined limbs.
I will call Her luck-bringer, for Her fingers are deft
at untangling the snares of a gnarled wyrd,
and sometimes the tangles are of Her making.
I will praise Her as strong in magic, cunning, skillful,
and battle-wise.
I will summon Her forth with song of steel,
for She is fierce and shows no mercy.
The field of combat is as sweet as the battlefield of love,
and in both, She is the victor.
She is sweetness and fury, molten flame, the sharp edge
of a killing blade.

She is danger and desire, unquenchable, unstoppable. She
will tease and entice, transforming the soul. She is
pleasure and pain so deeply bound there is no separation.
I hail Freya, Shining Goddess of the Vanir. She blinds
with Her beauty, seduces with Her fury.
I hail Her in Her fullness, in battle, witchcraft, and love.
I raise this horn in Her honor.
Hail, Freya!

Perhaps no other Goddess in Heathenry is so loved and also so often misunderstood as the Goddess Freya. She is an incredibly complex Goddess very often relegated solely to the realm of love and sex. She is most definitely a Goddess of sexual pleasure, eroticism, and desire, but She is also a Goddess of ritual sacrifice, seiðr magic, wealth, prosperity, abundance, ancestral veneration, warcraft, and power. These are not minor facets of Her nature either. So potent is Her prowess in battle that it is Freya, not Oðinn, who claims the first half of the slain warriors for Her hall. She is a gloriously beautiful Goddess and Her beauty is equal to Her power.

The name *Freya* means "Lady," but She has many other heiti including: Syr ("Sow"—the pig was a holy animal to the Germanic folk. It represented both battle prowess and fertile abundance. Freya shares this attribute with Her brother Freyr.), Mardoll (possibly "One Who Makes the Sea Swell"), Vanadis ("Lady of the Vanir"), Heiðr ("Bright One"), Horn (possibly "Flax"), and Gefn ("Giver"). Her home is called Folkvangr ("Field of the Folk"), and within it She maintains a great hall named Sessrumnir ("many-roomed hall"). She rides in a chariot drawn by some type of feline. Most Heathens assume these to be cats, but speculations range from cougars to lynx to wolverine. She is wed to Oðr, Who long ago disappeared. Nothing is known about Him, save that Freya travels far and wide searching for Him, weeping tears of gold or amber. (Amber is widely associated with this Goddess.) She has a daughter, Hnoss, whose name means "treasure." It could be said that Freya gives birth to wealth.

The most famous story about Freya involves the emblem of Her power and might: the necklace Brisingamen. Though most sources call

Brisingamen a necklace, there is some textual evidence that it may in fact have been a belt or girdle. Loki, who attempted to steal this piece of jewelry bears the heiti "the Thief of Brising's belt" but elsewhere the Eddas do refer to it as a necklace. The word *brising*, or *brísingr*, means "fire," which would lead to a possible translation of its name as "fiery belt." Some scholars link it to the aurora borealis; others see it as a symbol of Freya's fertility and sexuality. In order to win Brisingamen, Freya journeyed to the dwarven realm and commissioned a piece of such beauty and power that there would be none like it in all the world. The dwarves, master craftsmen, agreed to Her request but demanded in payment that She spend one night in sexual intercourse with each of them. This Freya did, and during those four nights, Brisingamen was forged. The necklace (or belt) is a symbol of Freya's power, just as Mjolnir embodies Thor's. It represents Her power to manifest desire on levels that go far beyond the sexual. She is less a Goddess of fertility and more that of synergetic attraction, which opens the doors to blossoming abundance. She is a Goddess of sensuality and of passionate fulfillment in life, be it giving one's all in love, in battle, or in pursuit of one's chosen crafts. She teaches us to suck the proverbial marrow out of life instead of drifting through it like a shadow.

Freya is the Patroness of unmarried women who go to Her hall when they die. She is also the priestess of the Gods, charged with maintaining the rites and making proper sacrifices for the Divine community. As seiðr worker, Freya is credited with bringing the practice of this form of magic, which involves trance work, mind control, and luck working to the Æsir. She was also, by Her very presence amongst the Æsir, a frith-weaver, having been sent from Vanaheim to secure peace with the Æsir.

Meditation for Freya

Set out a pretty piece of cloth—something that appeals to your personal aesthetics. It should be at least a foot square. Think about the many ways in which we define beauty in our culture. How do you, yourself, define beauty? What do you find beautiful? What nourishes you? What attracts you? What is beautiful about you personally? Do you think you are beautiful? Why? What would you change? Why? What would you sacrifice to be beautiful? Select an item that represents your beauty and place this on the cloth. This is an offering to Freya, a gift of gratitude and love.

How are you powerful? What would you do to fully manifest your personal power? Is this power a trait you admire about yourself? Is this part of your beauty? Select an item that represents your power and put that on the cloth as a gift to Freya.

How does Freya manifest in you? How does She inspire you? Does She make you uncomfortable? What gifts of abundance has She given you? Are there any areas that you feel particularly closed off to Her? Select a gift representing Freya's presence in your life, and add that to your bundle.

Add a piece of amber to the bundle, flowers, and anything else that you either associate with Freya or would like to give to her. Wrap the bundle up and secure it with ribbon. Take this to the nearest park, seashore, or any place in nature that is special to you. Call to Freya; speak to Her from the heart. Take as long as you wish. When you are finished, bury your offering, leave it by a tree, or cast it into the water with your thanks and a prayer of gratitude.

Loki

I will hail the Husband of Sigyn,
Father of Hella, Mother of Sleipnir.
I will greet Him with warmest welcome
to my Hall, this friend who has brought me success.
He has nourished me, succored me,
and brought me great comfort
in the deepest darkness, where no other could reach.
Shapeshifter, Skytreader, flame-haired Charmer,
My greatest blessings have come from Your hands.
Son of Laufey, Byleist's brother,
to me You have always shown Yourself true.
I praise You for all the many victories, great and small,
You have given me.

I offer praises to Loki, who has been my defender.
I offer praises to the One who is a friend to my House.

Loki is the most controversial Being in the entire Northern pantheon. To some, He is a Trickster Deity, capable of bringing change, evolution, and immense and surprising growth in the most unexpected of ways. To others, He is the enemy of the Æsir, the one who will lead the forces of chaos against the Gods at Ragnarokk. Many Heathens refuse to honor Him at all; to others He is a beloved Friend. A growing number of Heathens are incorporating the worship of the "Rokkr"—Jotuns honored as Gods of primal force, shadow work, and change. *Rokkr* is from a Norse word meaning "shadow" and encompasses such Deities as Loki, Hella, Angurboða, and Fenris. Loki is one of the most notorious members of this Divine tribe.

To begin with, Loki is blood brother of Oðinn. We are told in the Lokasenna that, in ages past, the two blended their blood together. This single act has puzzled scholars and caused endless consternation amongst modern Heathens, for this vow was an especially solemn one—a binding of souls, fate, and destiny. It was not an oath to be entered into lightly and was very nearly unbreakable. It is therefore unthinkable that Odin, a God who ordered the universe, a God charged with maintaining its integrity and balance, would bind himself to a trickster, a rule-breaker, a sly and cunning thief and finagler. Yet that is exactly what the surviving lore tells us He did. By doing so, Loki was welcomed into the company of the Gods.

Now, Loki certainly isn't a God who plays by the rules. He's not a God easily pigeonholed and He's not a God who will play within a votary's comfort zone. He strips all that away, demanding the right to act outside of any and all boundaries, like quicksilver flowing into every spiritual crevasse, every dark place where His touch is least expected. He is not a "safe" or comfortable figure and has a disconcerting tendency to alter all rules and mores to fit His own desires. Though the term is controversial when referring to Norse Deities, I would consider Loki a trickster in the same vein as Coyote or Ananzi. The word *fool* is often applied to trickster figures such as Loki, though it does not carry quite the same connotation as one might think. In the medieval period, the fool was often the only member of the court who could speak painful truths to the king without facing possible execution. As such, the fool, as an archetype, is a figure unhindered by societal constraints. However, one must explore exactly what the ultimate goal of any trickster's action is.

While it is true that Loki (indeed any God that chooses for Himself the role of trickster—and it is interesting but tricksters are almost invariably male) can create a state of extreme discomfort and annoyance, I would posit that if He shows up, there is always a reason for His presence. What may on the surface appear to be totally uncontrolled chaos can then be regarded as coldly calculated strategy, with the trickster as the vehicle of truth.

Loki is the enemy of entropy, of complaisance, and He fights it with a vengeance. He is the enemy of a heart without passion, devoid of devotion. He can be wrenchingly cruel to His children, but in hindsight, it is never *cruelty*, but rather the firmness of a parent to an erring child. And therein lies the secret to His motivation: He forces us to accept the full weight of our wyrd, to open to the myriad ways in which the Gods may inspire us, and to actively claim our own potential and the responsibility that comes with it. He can be a bastard, it's true (and I say this, loving Him dearly), but He's a bastard with a purpose.

Loki forces those who work with Him to expand the boundaries of their understanding. He brings evolution and a dynamic synergy and creative power. He acts as a catalyst and facilitator of personal growth. And with that growth may come the inevitable growing pains. The trickster is not an easy one to face or to accept, and not only because boundaries are irrelevant to Him. He forces us to examine in minute detail our own shadows, egos, and facades. He is the most powerfully kinetic instrument of truth, revealing what is meaningless and unhealthy in a way that is utterly pure, odd though it may be to associate purity with Loki. The inherent difficulty in this is the element of sacrifice integral to His nature. Interestingly enough, for all that the Trickster may challenge us in facing our own masks, that very role of "trickster" is but a mask that He himself dons. What lies beneath that varies: intense grief and pain, compassion, ecstasy, and a thousand other unexpected things.

Loki is a liminal figure, always existing betwixt and between, neither fully part of the world of the Jotuns nor fully part of the world of the Gods. Belonging to neither, He is able to move between both and possesses the synergetic power of active manifestation. Because he is a being of chaos yet bound to order via his oath to Odin, he is able to manifest this quixotic and change-inducing power directly in the ordered realm of the Gods. He opens careful doorways, and through them, that power is brought under tentative control. This liminality is perhaps the most ambivalent aspect of Loki's nature, though, if we look closely enough at the surviving lore, we see that Odin possesses it too.

Odin, however, always returns to the secure realm of inangard, to the hallowed ground of the Gods. Loki is never part of that, though He may dwell there for a while. He is always an outsider, always on the fringe of the Divine community.

Loki, ever existing in that liminal place where the numinous is made tangible, unites the mundane world of temporal order with the endless, fearless potential of the chaotic realms of power. He is a necessary figure, and the Gods knew this. Thor—the great defender of mankind, the God who is constantly at war with the forces of chaos, who girds the world against their intrusion—has a travelling companion on many of his quests. That companion is Loki. With his tricks and deceptions, Loki does precisely what Odin does: He brings power to the Æsir. But He doesn't do this directly. He creates discord, causes trouble, and then journeys forth (sometimes under threat) to find a solution to the trouble he has caused, and that solution almost inevitably results in greater power for the Gods. In fact, Thor received His mighty hammer Mjolnir, the symbol of his protective power, directly as a result of one of Loki's escapades.

Once upon a time, Loki, for reasons unknown, snuck into the sleeping chamber of Thor's wife, Sif, and cut off Her long, golden hair. In Norse society, a shorn head on a woman was the sign of an adulteress, so this was a grave insult. Thor was very, very angry and set off to avenge His wife. When He caught up with Loki, Loki swore that He would make everything as good as new. Thor, a bit dubious, let Him go but impressed upon Him the dire consequences if He failed to make good on His promise. So Loki journeyed to the best goldsmiths He knew of: the dwarves. He haggled, bartered, and finally induced them to make Sif a set of golden hair that would attach and grow like real hair, only a thousand times more beautiful. Given the gravity of His offense, Loki thought it best to return to Asgard with more than just new hair for Sif, so he goaded two different dwarven clans into crafting treasures for the Gods by insinuating that one could not best the other in skill. He then bet His head to the original dwarf, Brokk, that Brokk would lose the contest of skill. Loki returned to Asgard with Sif's new hair, which all the Gods agreed was even more beautiful than the original. He also brought back numerous other treasures, including Odin's spear and Thor's hammer, the latter of which, crafted by Brokk, won the bet. Just as Brokk was about to claim his reward (Loki's head), the quick-thinking trickster cried out that Brokk only had the right to His head, not any part of His neck. Of course it was impossible then to claim his reward, and the dwarf had to content himself with sewing Loki's lips together with thick sinew.

Much has been made of Loki's binding. After facilitating the death of Baldur by tricking the blind god Hoðr into throwing the fatal dart, Loki is captured and bound in a cave with the entrails of His own son. Many modern Heathens like to believe that Loki lies bound for all time, until the time of Ragnarokk, when the destiny of the Gods is at hand and the forces of order and chaos explode in battle once again. But though Odin bound him, He may also have given his bloodbrother one final gift. Odin controls the power of speech, represented in the rune Ansuz—unfettering power. Ansuz is a very unique rune: It is the attention and breath of Odin, and it washes away all that binds the spirit and the consciousness. It frees one to blend and unite with the Gods. Its Anglo-Saxon name translates as "mouth" or "God," and this is a very important clue to its true nature. To speak or to name something is to call it into being. This is one of the reasons why I believe the dwarves bound Loki's lips: to bind what He spoke, his power of manifestation. It's also worth noting that many of Loki's more memorable escapades involve His facility for scathing speech, which He was known to use, as in the "Lokasenna," to challenge everyone and everything.

Loki may lie bound on a slab in a dank, bleak cave, but nowhere is it ever recorded that his lips were sealed or his mouth gagged in this state (the lip-binding sinews of Brokk having been only temporary). He may be bound, but his voice, His power of manifestation, is not, and therefore *He* is not. In any discussion of Loki, the problem of Ragnarokk comes up. This translates as fate or destiny of the Gods and it is wise to remember that, in Norse thought, one had the power to alter one's fate. At the time of Ragnarokk, Loki is said to stand against the Gods. There is a certain cyclical order in this: chaos fighting order, as in the beginning. Many modern Heathens question whether or not Loki is even a God. He is of giant stock they say, an outlander, an intruder into the dynamic balance the Reginn[51] have created. He is chaos. He is the "enemy." But a little chaos is necessary for growth and evolution. Evolution is the heart-child of carefully chosen chaotic disruption and it is worth remembering that, in the beginning of the world, Odin gave soul and spirit to mankind. In sharing His blood with Loki, perhaps he shared something more: Godhood. Order may bring stability, but it takes a touch of chaos to bring forth change, growth, and even life. The presumed binding of Loki, the binding of all potential and opportunity, is inevitably followed by the destruction of Ragnarokk. Life cannot exist without a little chaos.

Loki is a very interesting Deity, regardless of whether or not one wishes to worship Him. He is a shape-changer and the only Norse God to repeatedly change not only shape but gender as well. Not only does He change into an old woman to prevent Baldr's return from Hella's realm, but He also changes into a mare and birth's Oðinn's steed, Sleipnir.

When Asgard was very young and the war between the Æsir and Vanir not long past, a man arrived with his horse, Svaðilfari. He presented himself as a builder and offered to build a wall so mighty around Asgard that hostile Jotuns would never be able to breach it. As payment, he wanted the sun and moon and for Freya to be his bride. Loki urged the Gods to accept but to set a condition of their own to ensure that the giant wouldn't win the loot that he wanted. The Gods agreed and stipulated that the wall must be finished by the first day of summer, thinking that surely even for the strongest of builders, this was an impossible task.

The builder accepted the deal and set to work, and as the weeks passed, the Gods grew more and more worried. The wall was rising with astonishing speed, and the first day of summer wasn't far off at all. If something wasn't done, the Gods were going to lose their wager. Because it had been Loki's suggestion to accept the builder's offer in the first place, the Gods rounded on Him and demanded that He fix the situation because, after all, the Gods weren't about to part with the sun, the moon, and, most importantly of all, Freya.

Loki observed the builder for a while and realized that he depended on Svaðilfari to haul the large blocks of stone; it was the horse's exceptional strength and speed that were enabling the builder to complete the job so quickly. The next morning, a delicate, long-legged mare appeared not far from where the horse and his master were working. She flirted with Svaðilfari, teased him, and finally led him on a merry chase, and the two of them disappeared for three days. The builder was unable to complete the project on time and, thus, forfeited his reward. He grew so angry upon realizing this that he showed his true face—that of an angry Jotun—and he began to destroy the wall, threatening the Gods as he did so. Thor took care of the situation with his hammer, slaying the giant.

Loki was absent from the ranks of the Gods for many months, appearing some time later with an eight-legged foal. This was Sleipnir ("Sliding One"), and he is named by Oðinn in the Grimnismal as the "best of horses." Oðinn claimed him for His own, and no word was spoken of who Sleipnir's mother was, for it was, in fact, Loki who had taken the shape of the mare to lure Svaðilfari away.

Loki has six children, actually. He is mother to Sleipnir, Father to Hella, Fenris, and the world-serpent Jormungand (with the giantess Angurboða), and Father to Narvi and Vali, sons by His wife Sigyn. Loki's own parentage is also known: His father is a Jotun named Fárbauti ("Cruel Striker"), often thought to be the personification of lightning, and His mother, discussed in a later section, is Laufey, also called Nál ("Needle," perhaps indicative of pine needles or tinder). He apparently has two brothers of which nothing more is known: Byleistr and Helblindi (which looks suspiciously like a heiti for Oðinn). There is much debate over the meaning of Loki's name. Some scholars speculate that it is related to words for *fire* or even *spider*, but nothing definitive had been agreed upon. Loki is seen as a God of fire, despite the fact that many of His transformations were into water creatures: the seal and the salmon. He has several heiti: Lopt ("the Airy One" or "the Lightening One"),[52] Sky-Traveller, Laufey's son, and Husband of Sigyn, to name but a few. Despite modern Heathen misgivings about Him, in the *Prose Edda*, He is "numbered among the Æsir."

Sigyn

I will hail Sigyn, gentle Goddess,
beloved wife of the Allfather's brother.
She is playful and sweet, sometimes shy,
yet fierce in Her own way, when She chooses to show it.
This unassuming Goddess holds weighty wisdom,
for those with ears to hear and eyes to see.
Her name speaks of victory and daring, boldness and power,
yet She is quiet and loving, simple in Her manner.
I will raise a horn to Sigyn; I greet Her with pride,
this Goddess who is far more than simply Loki's loyal bride.

Sigyn is mentioned exactly three times in lore. Each time refers only to the fact that She is Loki's wife and that, when He is bound after the killing of Baldr, She faithfully remains by His side, with a bowl, capturing the poison dripping from the venomous snake hanging above Him. When She empties the bowl and the poison falls on Loki's face, His painful writhing causes earthquakes. Many modern Heathens therefore dismiss Her as everything from merely a loyal wife to the epitome of an abused wife. She is seldom given the respect due a Goddess of Her integrity and strength. There is much more to Sigyn than initially meets the eye.

Sigyn is an exceptionally gentle Goddess. In fact, from my own experience of Her, I would say She is a shy Goddess, if that is possible, with an almost childlike innocence. The lessons that She brings have been no less transformative then Odin's, for instance, but She is gentle and playful about the entire process. Personally, I see Her as a Goddess of love and devotion. She is also the Goddess of the inner child and will heal that child within us. In fact, my very first experience of Sigyn was that of a playful child. I don't know why She chose to take that form, but it took me completely off guard. I experienced Her as a sweet and vulnerable child, a little girl who likes Her toys, likes to laugh, and wants to be loved—and Loki loves Her dearly. I was able to relate to Her in a way that I had never experienced with a Deity before: I felt protective of Her as a mother would to a child. Over the years, I have encountered other folk who honor Sigyn and Loki regularly, and they have also reported encountering Her in this manner.[53] Many also report experiencing Loki's extreme protectiveness of His bride as well, something that allows a rare glimpse into His compassionate, loving side that is little spoken of either in lore or by modern Heathens. Sigyn has the capacity to teach those who come to Her to open and embrace the Gods with the innocence and acceptance of a child. She too strips away the facades and walls and blockages within, but She does it so gently—so very gently—that it is a sweet embrace. She is a Goddess who opens the heart.

Of course there is another aspect to Her nature: that of the grieving bride who sits by Her tortured husband, doing what She can in the dank, bleak darkness of the cave to ease His pain. Here is a Sigyn who is fierce and strong, enduring as the rock and mountain, expansive and all-encompassing—a sanctuary in the face of suffering. Her name means "Woman of Victory," and that, alone, hints at Her hidden power. There is immense wisdom, caring, and compassion in this Goddess, and that is not something to dismiss lightly.

> Gentle Goddess,
> teach me to play.
> I've seen the joy You take
> in the smallest thing of beauty.
> Teach me gentleness,
> the sweetness of Your song.
> I want to sing, as You sing,
> when You know Loki is listening.

I wish to be among those nurtured
by Your tender hands,
a bright flower
pruned by Your gentle fingers.
Teach me to love,
as You love:
without condition.

Angurboða

I hail the great giantess,
Angurboða, Mother of Hella,
Mother of Fenris and the great serpent.
Great chthonic Mother, bless us with Your wisdom.
You are the dark, primal womb of all creation,
from Your bounty, the earth is filled with secrets.
You are the Silent One, Who bestowed upon
    Your daughter
all the magic of eternity.
In Your shadowy abode, You observed
the birth of the Æsir, and with Your magic,
You enticed Their brother Loki.
Great Mother of the beginning, bestow upon us
the silent endurance of rock and soil.
Let us always strive to see beneath the surface
of our dreams and desires for understanding.
Do not let us fall prey to pretty illusions
that sparkle and shine in easy imitation
of Your precious jewels; rather, grant us
the knowledge that wisdom need not be pretty
to be precious.
Come, Angurboda, smile upon us now.
We welcome Your blessings.

Angurboða is rarely honored as a Goddess amongst modern Heathens, yet She is included here because there is a small minority of modern worshippers who do choose to honor Her.

Her name means "One Who Brings Grief." Nothing is known of Her in lore, save that She was the lover of Loki and that, from Their union, three children were born: Hella, Goddess of the Dead; Fenris; and the great serpent Jormungand. Those who honor Her[54] call upon Her as a Goddess of great primal wisdom and fierce power.

Hella (Hel)

From the ice and shadow of Your obsidian abode,
You whisper to us.
You sit, carving runes of protection and defense,
knowing that, in time, all must journey to Your realm.
Your power, flowering like an ebon lotus fed by a
crimson tide
calls in dreams and sings in our blood.
Odin Himself bowed to Your wisdom,
writhing in agony on the Tree of sacrifice in exchange
for Your gifts.
Your name is so often spoken in hushed, fearful tones;
yet it is only knowledge
and comfort that You offer, a place of surcease and
learning.
There is no greater joy than to be blessed by Your
magic.
You sit in darkness, forging blades of power and
prophecy,
offering up Your gifts to those willing to call You
Mother.
Give me the strength to journey to Your dark places,
that I may learn from the hands that nestled me in
my mother's womb,
the hands that will gather my weary soul when my
mortal time is done.

I offer myself, that I may receive Thy burning kiss
upon my humble brow.
Hella, wrap me in the grace
of Your shadow. I hail You.

Hella is the daughter of Loki and Angurboða and ruler of the realm of the dead. All those who die of natural causes, old age, and sickness go to Her realm. While some accounts present it as a rather silent, dank place, it is not in any way a place of torment as in Christian ideology. It was a resting place for the dead, represented in the literature of the time as a great hall, analogous to the hall of any other God. Traditional sources give this Goddess a rather startling appearance: half black (decayed) and half white (living). Her realm was said to have nine levels, the lowest being Niflheim (although the remaining levels do not correspond to the other eight worlds connected by Bifrost bridge), to which the worst of the dead were confined.

The dankness and darkness so often associated with Helheim need not be seen as a negative. Burial mounds were sacred places, places to make offerings to one's honored dead, places to seek out their counsel. The mounds were even seen as doorways to the dead's afterlife dwellings. Hella's presence is one of stillness and incredibly kinetically charged stillness. It is stillness filled with a solitude that has color, texture, and a voice all its own. The dead are Her children and She knows the names of all who pass into Her hall. She is an ancient Goddess of immense patience and detached demeanor (at least in my experience and that of the various Hella's folk I have communicated with), yet at the same time, there is immense compassion there. All the wisdom inherent in the ancestral connection, all the knowledge of the dead, lies in Hella's hands. She is a Goddess of immense wisdom and power.

Committing to establishing a relationship with your own dead is an excellent way to begin honoring Hella. Setting up an altar to Hella or incorporating offerings to Her on an ancestral altar is an excellent way to begin honoring Her. I often give Her coffee and coffee beans in offering, as well as a rich Chambord. The dead must be honored before power can grow. We stand on the shoulders of our foremothers and forefathers, on the foundation laid by their struggle, hopes, dreams, and sacrifices. Their blood flows in us, we are formed from their very DNA, and that is the deepest, most primordial connection we could possibly have to the realm of this Goddess.

Laufey

Laufey, I wish to craft a beautiful prayer for You but words fail me in the face of the immense gift You have given me. You have returned to me my center, my roots, reconnected me to the Tree which is my strength and my foundation. I will praise You now and always.

I sense You in the quietness of the earth, the rich synergy of the crisp forest, wood supporting the flame, and the delicious spark of synapses and nerve endings that call our senses to life. You are the richness of the forest, green tranquility, its fire as it bursts into fierce delight at the first whisperings of autumn. You are the sweet, sweet silence that restores holiness to the damaged spirit.

You have renewed me, restored me, and returned me to the Gods I love when I was lost and hurting. I hail You, Mother of Loki. You have nurtured me like a daughter. My heart is bursting with gratitude for this unexpected gift. You have given me back reverent sight. Thank You, primal Mother. Thank You, my sanctuary. Thank You.

Laufey, also called Nál, is the Mother of Loki. I am only aware of a handful of Heathens who actively honor Her, however I have personally derived such benefit from Her kindness that I decided to include Her here. Her name means "leafy island," and Her secondary name, Nál, translates as "needle." Nothing is known of Her in lore, save the etymology of Her name, the name of Her husband, Farbauti ("Cruel-Striker"), and the fact that She is the mother of that most infamous of Gods, Loki.

She is sometimes seen as a Goddess of Trees, with Farbauti embodying the burning strike of lightning. I have experienced Her as immensely centering, yet with a definite heat, rather like the molten rock in the center of the earth—hidden from view but still powerful. There is an immense synergy about Her presence: it flows and crackles like tinder submitting to the flame, or the spark of electricity that causes synapses to fire and transmits sensory messages along the conduit of the nerve endings. Every time that I encountered Her, Her presence was very nurturing, like a mother bird guiding the chick in its first faltering flight. There was stillness and solitude, but through all of that a dancing rhythm—the sense of life existing in quiet harmony within the stillness. She is tranquility, and yet there is the sense of something immense, enormous, and ancient behind that benevolence.

Mimir (Meomer)

Wisest of Jotuns, Keeper of the well of memory,
I hail You.
All things hidden, all things secret, lie within
Your domain.
For Your wisdom, knowledge, and inspiration,
I praise You.
Friend of Oðinn, trusted Counselor,
I raise this horn in Your honor.

Mimir means "One who remembers," and He is very likely the uncle of Oðinn. It was Mimir and His sacred well at the spring Hvergelmir, in Jotunheim, to which Oðinn journeyed after His ordeal on the Tree. He asked for a draught from the well, because any who tasted of its waters would know all things. Mimir agreed, but only for a price: Oðinn had to pluck out His eye in exchange for His enlightenment. A single drink from Mimisbrunnr (Mimir's well) is a gift beyond price. As noted, Oðinn was not the only God to drink from Mimir's well. Heimdall also made the journey and attendant sacrifice (in His case, an ear) in exchange for exceptional hearing. One might speculate that the well contains the potential for every possible gift and wisdom, and only the willing sacrifice evokes its power, unique and individual to each God's desire. Another name for Yggdrasil is Mimameiðr: Tree of Mimir. Mimir is a God of cosmic memory,[55] wisdom, and deeply hidden power.

Rán and Aegir

I hail the Goddess of the ocean depths, Rán, Mistress of wealth and hidden secrets.
I honor You for the tumult and danger You bring.
I honor the personal clarity You bestow, with the painful precision of a harpoon sinking into the flesh.
I honor You, for Your memory is long; You see those things we mortals would forget, and You hold fast to what is Yours.
I hail You, Rán, Goddess of the Seven Seas, and ask for Your mercy.

I hail, Aegir, God of the Northern Ocean.
I hail You for Your bounty, for Your generosity, for Your wisdom.
I celebrate the wealth and mystery of Your watery realm.
I hail Your skill, delight of the Gods. I hail Your hospitality, which is celebrated in the halls of Asgard.
I hail You, Mighty Aegir, Bold Brewer of the Gods.

Rán is the Goddess of the sea and its depths. She hides its secrets and claims offerings from any who would make their living from Her realm. Drowning is essentially "falling into Rán's hands," and those who die in such a manner, particularly by drowning at sea, do not go to Hella's realm, but remain in Rán's realm of the dead. According to Simek, She embodies the sinister side of the sea[56] with its attendant danger. Conversely, She may also encourage the ocean depths to yield up its bounty to the sailor, the fisherman, and the treasure hunter. In my own experience, I have found that She tends to evoke immense, often traumatic and painful self-discovery in those who honor Her. She dredges up all the dark parts of ourselves that we might wish long buried and forgotten. Rán forgets nothing and, when we least expect it, will remind us of that we most wish to forget. She brings an astonishing clarity of mind, but it is the clarity of one who has accepted a death of the self, a death of old habits, behaviors, and states of being that no longer serve our growth. Rán's name means "Robber," for She owns a net that captures drowning people and draws them to Her realm. She is the wife of the sea-giant Aegir.

Aegir's name means "sea," and like His wife, Rán, He is a giant of the sea who often hosts the Æsir and Vanir in His hall. Given that He is so often referred to as a friend of the Gods, perhaps He may be honored as a God of celebration, hosting, and hospitality. Modern Heathens often honor Him for His brewing skills, and He has become the de facto Patron of modern home brewing.[57]

Other Deities

There are a number of other Deities worshipped by Heathens, both ancient and modern, who, due in part to the limited surviving lore, do not fit into any of the recognized tribes.

Hreðe

I say hail to Hreðe, Mighty Goddess!
With explosive force, You banish winter.
With enervating drive, You push us into
the rejuvenating arms of Spring.
Cleanse me, Glorious Goddess,
of all those things that hold me back.
Unfetter my mind, heart, and will,
that I might set my feet unswervingly on the road
to victory.
Hail, Hreðe, ever-victorious in every struggle!

Hreðe is mentioned only once in Bede's book *De Temporibus Ratione*. She is an Anglo-Saxon Goddess whose name translates as "The Glorious" or "The Victorious." The month of March in the old Anglo-Saxon calendar was named after Her, and She is perhaps best personified by the chill weather preceding the blossoming of Spring. There is some indication that She is a battle Goddess, given the etymology of Her name, but very little else is known.

I personally have a soft spot in my heart for this Goddess, being born at the tail end of March. I like to think that perhaps She can be said to embody the best characteristics of the Arien personality: forcefulness, immense creative drive, catalytic power, and a certain whimsical attractiveness.

Ostara (Eostre)

I praise Eostre, Goddess of the Dawn;
Rising mighty in the East, You bless us.
I praise Eostre, Goddess of the fertile fields.
With victory and fruitful luck, You nourish us.
I praise Eostre, Goddess of new beginnings.
With strength and resilience, You fortify us.
Shine Your light upon us, Holy Goddess.
Make our words and deeds mighty in Your eyes.
Replenish us daily with Your light.
We hail you, Gracious Goddess of the Dawn.
We hail You, Eostre, after whom Spring itself is named.
Please, Make us fruitful. Hail.

Ostara, or Eostre, is mentioned only once by Bede in *De Temporibus Ratione*, and despite the fact that one of the major Heathen holidays (the Spring Equinox) is named after Her—in addition to the Anglo-Saxon month of April—almost nothing else is known about this Goddess. It is known that the Christians gave Her name to one of their major holidays—Easter—and that much of the same symbolism currently ascribed to the secular celebration of Easter, such as rabbits and eggs, may also be given to Ostara as symbols of Her fertility and the awakening of the land.

She is a Goddess of springtime, governing all that entails: the rebirth of the land, the quickening of its natural rhythms, the lengthening of the days. She is a Goddess of new life; new beginnings; and young, newborn creatures. The impetus to reproduce may be Her gift as well. The egg is a potent symbol for Ostara (and the Spring Equinox, interestingly enough, is the only time an egg can be balanced on its end), as it contains the potential for new life, just like the land in the month that bears Her name. She brings about the warming of the earth after the ice and cold of winter.

Because Her name is connected to the Old High German words for "shining" and "east" and to the Greek "Eos" (Goddess of dawn in their pantheon[58]), many modern Heathens see Ostara as a Goddess of the dawn, in addition to being a Goddess of springtime, prosperity, and growth.[59] Her essence is best felt in the actual moment of the equinox, when Winter truly yields its hold on the land to Spring. She is potential in progress.

Personal Rite to Honor Ostara

The purpose of this simple rite is to celebrate Ostara's presence and to welcome Her blessings in your life. In addition to a faining, this is a nice way to celebrate Ostara. In late March/early April (as close to the actual Spring Equinox as possible), gather a number of seeds: flowers, herbs, vegetables—whatever you personally prefer. If you live in an apartment, you will want to purchase soil and planters so that this rite may be done inside, but if you actually have land or a yard, this should be done outside. Additionally, have a selection of edible seeds in a small bowl. Set up an altar,[60] either inside or outside, with the seeds, soil (if necessary), and any other images or items that you personally associate with Ostara.

Offer up a prayer to Ostara, inviting Her to witness and participate in this rite, offering its fruits to Her. The bowl of edible seeds represents potential and possibility. They are creativity that has not yet manifested, that which must be nurtured and cared for. They represent endless possibility of the spirit. Holding the bowl of seeds, spend a few moments meditating on what you wish to manifest in the coming year and speak this aloud. Ask for Ostara's blessing, and eat a few of the seeds. Ask for Her help in overcoming any obstacles and in remaining motivated. Set the rest of the edible seeds out in offering to Her, or sprinkle them outside as a gift for the birds.

Then take the seeds that you intend to plant. Prepare the soil, either putting potting soil in the containers that you will keep inside or preparing the actual ground outside to receive the seeds. With each seed (or handful of seeds, as many flower seeds are quite small), name aloud some blessing of Ostara's in your life that you are particularly grateful for.

Thank Her by giving something back to the land. When you are finished, spend as long as you wish meditating upon this Goddess. Then offer your thanks and go about your day. This rite should be done in the morning.

Saxnot/Seaxnéat

Sword Friend, strong as steel,
as loyal as a favored blade,
I hail You.
Your wisdom, from ages old,
flows in my very blood.
I will sing of You as my ancestors did.
Grant me wit and cunning wisdom,
strength of mind and heart and will,
Knife-keen focus, and a strong sword arm.
Ever will I hail You, Mighty God.
Ever to You, I pray.

Saxnot draws His name from the knife worn by Anglo-Saxon warriors, and His name translates as "Sword Friend" or "Friend of the Saxons."[61] Very little is known about this God but He was apparently once widely worshipped. Many modern Heathens consider Saxnot and Tyr to be the same God, others connect Him to Freyr. By His very name, He is often seen as an early Divine ancestor of the Saxon tribes. Saxnot, along with Thor and Woden, was specifically named and repudiated in a baptismal formula common to the ninth-century Saxons.

The Valkyrja (Wælcyrgie)

While not specifically Deities, these warrior women do figure prominently in Northern cosmology, particularly in the realm of soul-lore. Their name translates as "Choosers of the Slain," and They are the handmaidens of Woden. They occasionally protect His chosen heroes, keeping them from harm, but more often ride the field of battle, selecting particularly courageous fighters to join Odin's army in the halls of Valhalla. This army constantly trains in preparation for the final battle of Ragnarokk.

While later Germanic writings present the Valkyrja as beautiful women, civilized and wise, They were originally fierce warriors, enthralled with the fury and rage of battle. They are connected to the Nornir (Skuld occasionally being numbered among Them) in that They sever the life-threads of those heroes They choose. Regardless of whether the Valkyrja are seen as fierce, unstoppable warriors or wise and stately protectors, They reflect and embody the powers of the God to whom They are attached, Odin. They are often referred to as Shield-Maidens and occasionally as "Óskmeyjar": Wish-women (connected to Odin as Óski, Fulfiller of Wishes). Their individual names often reflect their role as Battle Maidens: Hild ("Battle"), Thrúð ("Din of Battle"), Randgríð ("Sshield Destroyer"), and Herfjötur ("Fetterer of an Army"), to name but a few.[62]

Mani (Mona)

I hail You Mani,
You are intoxicating in Your beauty.
You seduce with the promise of magic and
breathtaking stillness.
I hail Your power, subtle and secret,
the power of tides and blood and night-blooming
flowers.
I hail You for the memory of Your shining light
bathing my uplifted face.
I hail You for those moments when Your image,
lighting the darkened sky,
stole away my breath.
I hail You, shining, exotic, and glorious. For Your
mystery and Your allure,
I offer this horn.

Not much can be said about Mani other than that this God is the personification of the moon. According to Simek, He steers the moon and determines its waxing and waning.[63] He is the dark, subtle reflection of Sunna's radiant power. Two humans travel with Him on His nightly rounds: a girl named Bil and a boy named Hjuki. Mani is pursued by a ravenous wolf who will catch and devour Him at Ragnarokk.

Though little more is known about Him in lore, there are many ways to connect to this God. Simply going outside on a moonlit night and meditating on what qualities Mani's presence invokes is a good way to begin. In medieval herb lore, certain plants were sown and gathered at specific phases of the moon, so creating a garden of night-blooming flowers or sacred herbs is an excellent way for those with green thumbs to learn more about Mani. Women, of course, have a connection to His power through the rhythm of their menstrual cycles, which are ultimately governed by the cycles of the moon.

Sunna/Sigel/Sol

I hail Sunna, glorious in Her power.
It is Her life-giving warmth that nourishes and sustains us.
I give praise to this radiant Goddess. I celebrate Her glorious strength.
Without Her loving touch, our fields would wither.
Without Her gentle care, our world would be bleak and black.
I will praise Her gifts, more beautiful than amber, more precious than gold.
Hail, Sunna life-giver and protector!

Sunna, the Divine personification of the sun is rarely mentioned in the surviving lore. There is a reference to Her in the Merseburg Charm and in the Eddas. Like Mani, She was drawn across the sky in a chariot pulled by two horses and pursued by a hungry wolf. She was venerated by early Germanic peoples as a life-giver. It was Her power that helped the crops to grow, providing sustenance for a people who lived in a cold, often inhospitable land. She governed the cycle of day, and the rhythms of agricultural life largely revolved around Her rising and setting. Today we can honor Her as our Pace-setter, as most of us still rise to begin our workday by Her unchanging cycles. She may be invoked to bring rejuvenating power to us during our day, and her mere presence provides a constant reminder of the Gods' presence and power in our daily lives.

Jorð (Eorðe)

Hal wes þu, folde, fira modor!
Beo þu growende on godes fæþme,
fodre gefylled firum to nytte.
Wassail Earth Mankind's mother;
Be growing in God's embrace,
Filled with food, man to joyously help...[64]

Jorð is the personification of the earth itself. She is the daughter of Night, lover (possibly wife) of Odin, and the Mother of the great God Thor. Throughout the lore, She is known by many different names: in Old Norse she is called Fjörgyn[65], Hlóðynn, Fold ("Earth"), and Grund ("Ground"). In Old English she is called Folde and Fira Modor ("Mother of Mankind"). She is a Goddess of nourishing power, fearsome might, and all-encompassing strength. Because of Her benevolence, fields flourish, flowers grow, and fruits ripen. Because of Her, mankind is able to draw sustenance from the land. Her might shines forth in the earthquake, the hurricane, and the tornado. The cycle of seasons centers around Her. She is the foundation and keeper of untold wealth: land, mountains, minerals, oceans, trees, foliage, crops. An excellent means of honoring Her in our world today is to commit to mindful consumption and recycling or ongoing volunteer work at a local park.

Holda/Frau Holda/Holle

Hail, Frau Holda, I honor You and the secrets
You hold.
I ask that You teach me Your wisdom, Mother
of the Hunt.
I have seen You, magical, impish, mischievous...both
fierce and gleeful as You share Your knowledge.
I would learn from You. I will bring patience and
industry to the task.

I will not falter or back away from the unknown to which You hold the key. I will be steadfast and bold, I promise You. I will work with focus and care to integrate Your teaching into my life. I welcome Your transformation. I hail You now, Frau Holda. Please accept this offering of wine from my hand. Hail.

Some Heathens see Holda as a hypostasis of Frigga; after all, Woden has His numerous disguises, so why should Frigga be any different? Others connect Her strongly with Hela, and still others see Her as a Goddess in Her own right. In Germanic folklore, She appears alternately as a motherly Goddess, rewarding industry and hard work with great blessings of abundance, or as the fierce leader of the Wild Hunt (along with Woden), Queen of Witches, and collector of souls—particularly the souls of dead children. Her realm is traditionally believed to lie beneath the earth, inside mountains, or even beneath lakes and ponds.

Nehellenia

Hail, Ancient Mother, Goddess of the primal waters,
Goddess of ships and of abundance.
You bridge the gap between the living and the dead,
You carry our offerings to the hands of our ancestors.
You carry our prayers to the ears of our honored dead.
You are Goddess of life and of death, and all passages are aided by Your nourishing hands. I hail You, Ancient Mother.

Nehellenia is a Dutch Goddess honored on numerous votary stones and altars dating from the third century C.E. Many of these altars show depictions of fruit offerings, ships, and dogs, and there is some evidence that Her worship had much in common with that of the Egyptian Goddess Isis, whose worship was carried to the Northern shores by Roman invaders. According to Simek,[66] Her name may mean alternately "Goddess of Death,"[67] "Goddess of seafaring," or "the helpful Goddess coming close." Given the symbols of both fertility and death so strongly associated with Her, She is honored today as a Goddess of passages.

This is hardly an exhaustive list of Germanic Deities. There are many lesser-known Gods and Goddesses who are not included here, including Alateivia; Haeva; Viridecdis; and Oðinn's sons, Vali and Vidar, who take vengeance on His behalf. Though little is known about how They were all worshipped in elder times, the door is open for modern Heathens to rediscover the power and nature of these Mighty Gods.

Chapter 4

Wyrd

One of the most important and complex facets of Heathen theology is the concept of wyrd. Awareness of wyrd and its power underlies the structure of both religious and social interactions within the Heathen community. In many ways, wyrd may be likened to fate, but it is far more interactive. It encompasses the sum total of one's individual actions and choices, as well as whatever destiny may have been predetermined by the Nornir for that individual. It is the esoteric unification of all that was and all that will be, manifesting in temporal life. Wyrd is both causality and consequence, and it constantly changes and shifts. It is a web of choices: one's own choices, the choices of others, the choices of one's community, and even the choices of one's own ancestors impacting his or her current evolution and awareness.

Wyrd orders the multi-verse. Even the Gods must bow to the power of Their own wyrd. Within Heathen theology, the Gods are not omnipotent; They are bound, just like mankind, by the power and pattern of wyrd. Its pattern and flow is the one constant immutable law governing every aspect of existence. Humanity's relationship with wyrd is reciprocal; our lives are governed by its law, yet the various layers of that law are laid in accordance with the choices and actions of our lives. We create and must abide by our own fate. The action of wyrd is analogous to a pool of water: Cast a stone, ripples form. If five people each cast a stone at the exact same time, those ripples overlap. The fish swimming below the surface create eddies that may also affect the smooth surface of the pool. Even the wind may affect the water. The more immediate someone's involvement with the individual, the more of an effect it has on that individual's wyrd. The pool of water represents the world, and the concentric rings indicate the distance and effect of influence of every person one meets. One's individual strand of wyrd, the part that each person has the power to affect for good or ill, is called *orlog*.

In *The Well and the Tree*, the seminal work on the Norse concept of fate, Paul Bauschatz writes that "there is little doubt about the central importance of the world tree as a symbol of a large part of the universe as conceived by early Scandinavian people."[1] Indeed it is a central theme in Heathen Cosmology—the fundamental supporting structure of the worlds of Gods and man. Its very prominence in the cycle of myths points strongly to a highly evolved system of Shamanic practice, for the Tree is nearly ubiquitous in the annals of world culture as a means of transport to other, unseen worlds.[2] But even more important than the Tree is that which rests amongst its roots: Urtha's Well.

In the Voluspa,[3] it is clearly stated that the Nornir craft and decree the laws of mankind. They "set or mark fate"[4] and speak orlog. The very etymology of this word, *ur*, marks it as something primordial and ancient, something of essential import, fundamental to all that is. In the setting of orlog, the Nornir lay the foundational bricks in the road of spiritual evolution. They create a place where echoes of the past meet echoes of the future. All that was, is, or shall ever be is contained within the depths of Urtha's Well. More importantly, because our own fate is laid down in this place, it is the nexus of our connection to our ancestral path, the connection of our deeds and choices to those that came before and will come after. It is our primal memory, and memory is a very precious thing. Odin has two ravens as companions, one named Muninn, the other Huginn. He sends them out daily to observe and bring back information. Odin cherishes Muninn (memory), fearing its loss even over Huginn (thought).[5] The Greeks (to whose *Moirai* Bauschatz compares the Nornir) considered memory and wisdom inseparable and personified them both in the essence of the Goddess Metis. Shamans were, in part, the memory keepers of their communities.[6] A healthy community is founded on the organic evolution of tradition that flows from that wellspring of memory. This is one of the reasons that modern Heathens are so insistent about basing the reconstruction of their religious practices and social structure on the surviving remnants of the pre-Christian world. Memory defines who and what we are, and to *remember* is to recall ourselves to ourselves. This recollection is echoed in the daily setting of law by the Nornir, and that daily repetition recalls to life our own deeds, our spiritual evolution, the growth (or not) of our character, and the enduring wisdom of our dead.

Memory nourishes humankind and restores to us an awareness not only of the foundations of the world but of the proper order of things. Much of that awareness is in the hands of our ancestors. All of that awareness and knowledge is contained in the Well. It lies concealed within the very layers of action and orlog and of choices laid upon choices that define our fate. And this has the power to connect us, as nothing else can, to the dead, upon whose shoulders we stand. It inspires and connects us not just to the memory of our blood kin, but to the memory of the very earth upon which we live, the memory of the Tree itself, the memory of the incarnations of our own souls, and even to the fabric of which the universe was made. Here is our essential mystery: the Well and the Tree that is nourished by it. Here is our starting point.

The Well and the Tree form a point of "intersection" between this world and the "world beyond."[7] It is the place where all choice and consequence meet. There is a reason that the Allfather had to hang on the World Tree to gain access to the runic mysteries: only beneath its boughs, in the Well of being itself, could He find the keys to *wyrd* and its unfolding. But, just as actions have consequences, so do choices have cost: that which will become. As memory and order are contained within the sphere of Urtha, so the price of knowledge, decision, and sacrifice are contained within the realm of Skuld.[8] An analysis of the name *Skuld* reveals that it denotes necessary action—even constraint and obligation. Therefore, it could be said that memory and action carry with them obligations.

Wyrd and orlog are not, then, abstract concepts, but something contained in the very fiber of our bodies, minds, and spirits—encoded in our metaphysical DNA, just as our height and hair color are encoded in our physical DNA. The individual threads of orlog, those laws so diligently laid down beneath the Tree, are the very molecules from which our lives are formed. We even inherit part of our wyrd and its attendant obligations from our ancestors. Evolution is the sphere of Verdande. All three names of the Nornir bear connotations of evolution of time as a repetitive and circular process.[9] In other words, time flows in on itself and from itself, bound by the fabric of memory. It is not in any way linear; it is only our perceptions that make it so.[10] The Nornir are thus "out of time," not bound by the constraints of that evolution.

Urtha is solid. She is that which is ordered and manifest. She sets the boundaries in which our fate will be created and played out. Verdandi orders our actions, weaving them into the warp and weft of those boundaries, even as we make them. Skuld binds us to the consequences of our choices for good or ill. We choose what we give to Her, but once given, we are bound by our choice. Everything, however, begins with Urtha. In Her is contained the sum total of all experience; She stands before being[11] just as She stands after it. It is this common origin and terminus that, more than anything else, stands in stark opposition to the extreme rugged individuality that is so encouraged within modern Asatru. Yes, we are responsible for our own actions but, at the same time, we are connected, through Urtha's Well, to each other. At some point, it all returns to the Well. To quote Bauschatz: "Urtha unfolds the pattern and sequence of all events as they build up and out into the present world; she illustrates the fundamental importance of the orlog, the 'primal' events laid down in earliest times, whose pattern dominates and structures events now occurring in the world of men."[12] This is our ancestral memory, that which forms the shades and structure of our Hamingja, our ancestral luck.[13] In other words, part of each of our souls rests in the Well beneath the Tree.[14]

The nature of the Well hearkens back to the primal substance contained in Ginungagap and the impulse which triggered creation. It is apropos that the sacred substance be conceived of as water. Water is quixotic and changeable. It can seep into every crevasse, no matter how small. It transforms and transmutes itself from ice to snow, steam to liquid, yet always retains its essential structure. It is necessary to life and constitutes 80 percent of our bodies. It is indispensable. Bauschatz notes that the water of Urtha's well was "water of a special, active quality"[15] and the "Gylfaginning"[16] specifies it to have purifying power. Our lore tells us that the water heals the Tree, the macrocosm of all reality. The Tree is the direct manifestation of all that is contained within the Well. The Well contains the past and the power it brings to the Tree is the power "the past has over all of present existence."[17] It is symbolic of a very precise alchemy, a collaboration of often dichotic elemental forces that have the ability to shape or destroy the world.

More importantly, "the process of occurrence of events and the continual accumulation of more and more of them into the pattern of the past present a system of growth that is never finished."[18] This is very important. This cyclical nature of the interaction of the Well and the Tree reflects the pattern that plays out in our spiritual journey as well. It defines the "interrelations of all actions."[19] As the water of the Well provides nutrition and healing to the Tree—literally to the structure and support of our world—it may be surmised that memory provides nourishment to our spirits. We are defined by what we remember and it is the constantly shifting, interrelating layers of memory that nourish our spirits. Urtha will "lead one to wisdom."[20]

Chapter 5

The Soul Matrix

Within Heathenry, the soul is conceived of not as a single, undivided entity but as a composite of parts, a microcosm of the immense and varied macrocosm of the multi-verse in which we live. The soul constitutes a matrix of interrelated and interdependent sections, each with its own realm of influence, its own power, and its own impact on one's life. To be healthy, hale, and whole, the entire matrix must be kept strong and in balance. The strength and vitality of each part of the soul matrix may be impacted by the honor of one's actions (or lack thereof), the mindfulness with which one attends to holy duties, one's devotional life, one's ancestors, the way in which one chooses to live his or her life, and one's wyrd. It is, in many respects, the field on which the patterns of wyrd take potent life.

Typically, the soul may be seen as having between nine and 12 parts (some denominations combine several of the soul sections listed on the following pages). It makes sense for the soul to be comprised of multiple facets; as humankind was created by the gifts of three Gods—Oðinn, Hoenir, and Loður—so the structure of our souls reflects Their triune power. While it is necessary to dissect the soul matrix to gain a thorough understanding of how each part functions, it is even more important to recognize that the true power lies in the ever-evolving balance of the working whole.

The Lík/Lich[1]: The Physical Body

Surprisingly, the physical body is considered the most basic part of the soul. It is the vehicle of our incarnation, through which our wyrd plays out. It is the vehicle through which we are able to enact our will, the will of the Gods, and our highest destiny, as well as to resolve our wyrd-debts. It is also the means by which we experience the world directly and by which we leave our mark. Honoring the body is a vital part of maintaining a healthy soul. It is the vessel of one's personal power. Maintaining a sense of mindfulness over eating healthily; exercising and keeping fit; and pursuing martial arts, sports, dance, and yoga all help us strengthen the Lík. Additionally, when working with this soul part, it is important to carefully examine the attitudes toward our bodies, physical strength, and even sexuality and gender roles that we may have picked up from the dominant culture. In fact, it is important for newcomers to Heathenry to consciously set about exploring and examining their attitudes toward every aspect of their world at large.

Every day we are bombarded by thousands of unconscious, subconscious messages, and very few of them reflect the values and ethics of Heathen culture. Heathens value physical life and take great pride in their accomplishments in this area. There is no dichotomy between spiritual and physical, as might be found in other Western religions. Rather, one flows seamlessly into the other, and the holy is found as easily in one's daily life, work life, and romantic life as it is in the most moving of religious rites. Because the physical body is part of the soul, if one's attitudes toward the body aren't healthy, then the soul itself cannot be healthy. Looking at the structure of the soul, it can clearly be seen that the body, mind, and emotions are interconnected. Working to heal and strengthen any one part will have positive effects on the whole.

Önd/Aeðem: The Divine Breath

Önd, or Aeðem, is that which animates the soul. It is our connection to the Gods—the breath of Oðinn, breathed into us at the moment of the soul's creation. It is what gives us life and consciousness and the ability to grow and evolve. It is our connection to the Gods, our elder Kin. Each breath we take calls to mind that sacred connection. The Önd is the part of the soul that is in constant connection with the Gods and the cosmic unfolding of our spiritual evolution. It connects us to the "bigger picture" if you will.

Hamingja: Luck

The Hamingja is one's personal luck. It may be nourished or diminished by our actions and choices. It is a vital, living, ever-changing thing—one that we are constantly creating. In many ways, our Hamingja determines the quality of our lives, the degree of difficulty we will have to expend to reach our goals, and our chances of success. A certain degree of luck is inherited from our ancestors and the result of their choices, actions, victories, and struggles. It flows from the mother to the child and, like our very DNA, connects us to those who have gone before and those that will follow us. We are charged with living rightly so that our own Hamingja will leave no debt for our children to work out. There are many ways of strengthening and increasing one's personal luck. The strength or weakness of our Hamingja can affect us in many intangible ways—not only with lack of personal success, but also with physical illness, depression, and emotional crisis. Living honorably, keeping one's sworn word, paying mindful attention to one's personal obligations, giving back to one's community, honoring one's ancestors, and striving to better oneself are all good places to begin. It goes hand in hand with one's *Maegen*, or vital force.

Maegen: Vital Force

Maegen is the vital force that flows through every living thing. It is intimately connected with one's luck and, like the Hamingja, may be directly impacted by the way in which we live our lives. Dishonorable choices, the breaking of one's word, doing harm to kin and community, or living in a way that brings harm to oneself all indirectly weaken one's vital force. Whereas luck is affected directly by our actions, those same actions cannot affect the vital energy itself. What those actions affect is our ability to be a strong container for that force. It allows us to tap into (or not) a greater degree of vital power. Maegen is comparable to what Eastern religions call "ki" or "chi," and it allows us to act in the world. It is this that gives us the power to alter our wyrd and strengthen or weaken our luck and power. It may be seen as fertility of the spirit. Maegen, like Hamingja, may be increased or diminished by the quality of our deeds. Maegen is like a generator, a reservoir of power that keeps us hale, healthy, and whole. Strengthening the will, the Hamingja, and the Lík all contribute to maintaining a strong Maegen.

The Willa: The Will

The Willa is the vehicle by which we assert our desires on the world at large. It is a direct expression of our personal power, which inspires our talents, creative drive, intellect, and passions. It is the means by which we reach our goals and impact the world around us. Like the other parts of the soul matrix, the will must be balanced between desire and intellect, duty and wyrd, the good of the individual and the good of the tribe/community as a whole.

Hugr/Hyge: The Intellect

The Hugr is our intellect, our capacity for rational thought. It is this part of the soul matrix that gives us our cognitive functions and our ability to make sense of our experiences. It enables us to learn, grow, and process our interactions with each other and with the world at large. It is this capacity for rational decision-making that enables us to live rightly and choose to impact our communities in a positive way.

Mynd/Minni: Memory

It might seem strange to find memory included in the soul matrix, but this particular aspect of the soul was so precious to the Germanic tribes (which were primarily an oral culture) that the God Oðinn worried more about the loss of memory than about the loss of His ability to think cogently. Memory is what connects us to our tribe, our self-definition, our ancestors, and our own evolution. It is our foundation, and it nourishes our growth and strength, much like a tree's roots ensure its survival. It enables us each to celebrate our uniqueness and our identity and to learn from past experiences. Swain Wodening, in his work *Hammer of the Gods,* posits a connection between the function of memory and our ability to care for and love another.[2] Both the intellect and the memory are personified by Oðinn's two ravens: Huginn (Mind) and Muninn (Memory).

Oðr/Wod: Passion, Ecstasy, and Inspiration

Just as intellect is part of the soul, so is our ability to feel passion. This isn't necessarily *sexual* passion, but a drive and determination to excel. It shows forth in devotion, inspiration, and excellence. It is our ability to give ourselves fully to an endeavor without hesitation or compromise. The Wod is responsible not only for the creative inspiration of the poet and artist but also for the raging destructive power of the berserkr warrior. Inspiration was often believed to go hand in hand with madness and frenzy, which gives some indication of what occurs when this part of the soul is nourished by itself, without being properly integrated into the functioning whole. Facing one's inner demons, dealing with any unresolved issues, facing our fears, shadow work—all of these things help to encourage balanced expression of one's personal Wod.

Fylgja/Fæcce: Guardian Spirit

The Fylgja is one's guardian spirit and may often appear in animal form as a power animal or as a being of the opposite gender. The Fylgja assists in helping us to reach our full potential. Through its guidance, we are able to tap into our personal power, and it is generally believed that the Fylgja aids us in fulfilling our wyrd and governs the distribution of Maegen and flow of Hamingja. Working directly with the Fylgja can lead to amazing insights and inspiration. Often one's Fylgja may appear or communicate through dreams but can also be directly contacted through meditation.

Orlog/Orlæg: Personal Wyrd

Wyrd itself, as we have already discussed, is the web of all being, constantly being woven and rewoven. Orlog is one's individual strand within that greater conglomeration of threads. It is this part of the soul that connects us to that greater web and it is this strand that we have the ability to directly affect. Orlog is the field upon which our decisions take shape, affecting our Hamingja, Maegen, and lives.

Hamr/Hama: Etheric Soul Skin

Edred Thorsson, in his book *Runelore*,[3] speculates that the Hamr is the power of imagination that can, at times, take active shape and form in our world. More commonly, it is thought of as a type of soul-skin, which contains the various parts of the soul matrix and which we might shape and direct according to our will. Norse literature is replete with stories of sorcerers going into trances and sending forth their Hamr to work their will. Oðinn Himself is said to possess this ability. The Hamr gives us the ability to journey forth and to act in other worlds, realms, and states of being.

Mod: Self-Consciousness

Essentially, the Mod is the self, that part of the soul that is incarnated in the here and now, containing all that we are—our awareness, consciousness, and temporal being. The Mod is "a reflection of the integrated self"[4] and of a properly integrated soul matrix.

It is obvious from the nature of the soul matrix that Germanic theology did not (and does not) contain a split between this world and the spiritual world. The two were intimately connected, equal partners. One could not truly succeed in the spiritual by neglecting the physical or in the physical by neglecting the spiritual. The two aspects of being flowed into and from each other. Living well meant living in a way that benefited not only oneself but one's community, as well; it meant living with honor.

The Germanic Concept of the Afterlife

Heathen Cosmology has no concept of heaven and hell comparable to what is found within the Judeo-Christian religious paradigm. There were several destinations a soul might take after physical death. Just as

Heathen Cosmology shares a belief in multiple worlds, so the afterlife is believed to consist of several realms, as well. Death is not in any way thought to be the end of existence, nor is it a static, unchanging state of being. The soul of the newly deceased has options.

In simplest form, it may be said that life continues after death, in the realm of the ancestors, much as it does in temporal life. Ancient Heathens would erect elaborate burial mounds over the graves of their ancestors, and offerings would be left there to honor the dead. Those seeking wisdom would spend the night at the howe,[5] and often their perseverance was said to be rewarded, as their ancestors came forth to speak directly to their descendants. The howe was in many ways considered a doorway to the realm of the ancestors, and the dead were by no means locked away from the world of the living. Female ancestors (called *Dísir*, or singular, *Dís*) were especially influential in the life of the living family, and stories abound about powerful Dísir warning their descendents of danger and sharing wisdom and advice, often appearing in dreams to do so. Those who die of natural causes—sickness or old age—go to Hella's realm. This is in no way a place of torment, but rather a great ancestral hall where the dead reside. Some modern Heathens believe that particularly vile people will end up in Nastrond, a dank pit in the lowest, darkest region of Hel. With the exception of Nastrond, Hel is not an unpleasant place.

Those killed in battle, by bladed weapon, or in special service to the God Oðinn were said to dwell in Oðinn's hall, Valhalla—a hall of warriors, where the chosen few continued training so that they would be ready to fight the final battle of Ragnarokk. Oðinn was often said to meddle in the affairs of mortals to hone his chosen warriors, eventually setting in motion events that would lead to their death at the height of their strength and power. (It's important to realize that His ultimate goal is ensuring the continued survival of both humanity and the Gods.) Half of the fallen warriors go to Freya's hall, as She has first pick of the slain. Death in battle was considered preferable to death of old age or disease, and the Germanic peoples were fierce fighters because of this. The host of Oðinn's hall were called the Einherjar, and many modern Heathens conduct special fainings in their honor on Veteran's Day and Memorial Day. Military service is still considered a great honor amongst modern Heathens, and those who serve either in the military or as police or firefighters have places of honor within the community.

Today we live in a world far different from that of our ancestors, and it is no longer likely that we will die in actual combat. Therefore we must look at the attitude and mindset of the warrior to see what we can glean from this. Living honorably; holding to one's word; committing to a set of values; doing what is right, even in the face of fierce opposition; being willing to defend oneself and one's loved ones; standing up for what is right; rejecting complaisance, cowardice, and moral relativism; and constantly striving for excellence in every area of life—all of these things are ways in which we can live a warrior's life today. Doing what is right, even when it is most difficult; speaking out and speaking up when necessary; being forthright in one's dealings; and avoiding those actions, however small, that diminish us as people are all actions of a warrior and all ways that we can connect with our honored dead.

Those who died by drowning belong to the Sea Goddess Rán and are believed to be drawn down into Her realm by Her fishing net, which none thus caught may escape. Those who die devoted to a specific God or Goddess may go to that Deity's hall after death. Of course, the spirit may choose to remain and watch over his or her family, lending strength, wisdom, and protection. The important point to remember is that the dead have options. Many Heathens even believe in reincarnation: that the souls of the dead are born again and again into the temporal world. Unlike Eastern beliefs of reincarnation, Heathens do not believe that the soul may take animal or plant form. Most believe that the dead will reincarnate within their family line.

Honoring the Ancestors

In many traditional cultures (including the pre-Christian Norse and Germanic cultures), it was generally believed that the living had certain obligations to the dead. Where these obligations were properly and respectfully fulfilled, luck, wealth, blessings, and abundance would fall upon the family, and they would have powerful allies in the unseen world.

Where those attendant obligations were neglected, the entire living family would suffer. One of the most painful aspects attendant to the spread of Christianity across the world has been the severing of those ancestral ties, the neglect, and at times, the open vilification of such practices. Strength, luck, and vitality come from the ancestors. We stand on the shoulders of our dead; their struggles, hopes, sacrifices, and even their errors have contributed to the quality of our own lives and who we are today. We need not know their names to honor them. The dead, no matter how far back in one's ancestral line, know their children. The Álfar (male ancestors) and Dísir (female ancestors) maintain an interest in their family line.

Ancestral veneration is an instinctual practice that even 2,000 years of Christianity has not erased. Though our culture has done everything it can to remove the sacred from the deathing process, we still visit graves, keep pictures of our loved ones displayed, name children after deceased relatives, and tell their stories. To those who have returned to the practice of their indigenous religions, such as Santeria, Lukumi,[6] Native American Spirituality, and Heathenry, honoring the dead is taken a step further. We feed the dead, setting out great feasts; we talk to them, include them in major family decisions, call upon their wisdom and strength in times of trouble, and communicate with them frequently, taking heed of their advice. They remain vital and active members of the family. An awareness slowly develops of being one gleaming pearl in a strand of pearls stretching back to the beginning of time and endlessly into the future. Our connection in the ongoing thread of ancestors becomes part and parcel of our daily consciousness. It is a palpable awareness that governs every action. Even for those who have chosen not to have children, they still take their place in the web of ancestors as guides, teachers, examples. One does not have to be a blood relative to be honored as an ancestor. There are connections of spirit that are equally powerful to—in some ways more powerful than—those of blood.

None of us come into this world alone; we come with a line of ancestors, foremothers and forefathers stretching back untold generations. If we can do nothing else to reclaim our sacred traditions, to build again strong, autonomous communities, we can honor our progenitors. A life spent with mindful awareness of that holy connection is a life well lived. Speak their names. Tell their stories. Research their cultures. Learn their languages. Research your own genealogy. Visit graves. Set up an altar to your dead. Bring them gifts. Bring them your attention as an ongoing devotional act. For those who are adopted, you have two sets of ancestors to celebrate—those of your blood family and those of your adopted family. It isn't necessary to know their names. Simply make the call and they will know you. For those who come from abusive families, reach further back or call upon spiritual ancestors—those people and perhaps heroes who inspired and taught you on your journey. There is no shame and much power in such an act. Opening the door to one's honored dead opens the door to a reservoir of support, knowledge, and personal might unimaginable to those who live with their eyes on the living world alone. It restores the sacred to the deathing process. It restores the sacred to our communities. It nourishes our spirits. Even more than honoring the Gods Themselves, venerating one's ancestors is a fundamental building block of Heathen practice.

Ritual for Honoring the Ancestors

For those who have never worked with their dead on an ongoing basis, for whom the concept of ancestral veneration is a new one, setting up an ancestral shrine provides an excellent time to begin the process of reconnecting to one's lineage and forebears.[7] Many indigenous cultures have their own methods of doing this, but I will share the one that has worked for me—one that is fairly common within Heathenry: that of the ancestral altar and feast.

Begin by setting up an altar. It doesn't have to be elaborate, but it should be separate from your devotional altar. A windowsill or bookshelf will do. I know a woman who has four cats. She simply cannot keep a regular altar, so she has constructed a reliquary box. Her altar is contained within a large carved box. When she wishes to honor her ancestors, she opens the box, sets out her offerings, and talks to her grandmother. She doesn't leave the offerings out, but commits them to the earth after she is finished. Adapt the practice of altar meditations in whatever way best suits your individual lifestyle. Form is less important than the act of mindful contemplation itself. Choose where and how you will construct your altar. Many traditions, such as Lukumi, often use white altar cloths and white flowers, with nine glasses of water on their altars. I too have found this helpful. Creating an ancestral altar is an act of hospitality. You are inviting your ancestors not only into your house, but into your life. By setting out water, you provide them with symbolic refreshment, as you would any guest.

Once you have decided where you want your altar to go, begin by consecrating the space in whatever way is common in your spiritual tradition. Offer incense and a prayer to the Goddess of the Underworld (Hela), asking that She help facilitate communication in your new endeavor. The prayer, like the action of crafting an altar, should come from the heart. Once you feel Her presence strongly, begin constructing your altar, verbally speaking aloud the reason you are including each object.

Anything can go on an ancestral altar that reminds you of that sacred connection: pictures of the dead, if you have them; items from the culture in which your ancestors lived (for instance, I use an altar cloth that was hand-woven in Lithuania to represent the generations of Lithuanian ancestors on my father's side, about whom, sadly, I know nothing); a genealogical chart; flowers; incense; elemental symbols, if you like; objects belonging to your dead—these are just suggestions. Each altar will be as individual as the person constructing it. Spiritual ancestors and heroes should absolutely be included here.

Once your altar is constructed, spend as much time as you like meditating in front of it. When you feel ready, call to your ancestors. If you know their names, call them by name, welcome them into your life, and explain what you are doing and why. I realize that many of our ancestors will be Christian or Jewish or Islamic. That's okay. It's the honoring that is important, not what religious tradition they followed. This is not about which God or Goddess we worship, but about reconnecting with one's family and the source of one's strength.[8] Ask them to be a part of your life again, and tell them that you will be honoring them regularly. If a dead relative was abusive to you, he or she need not be honored. I have seen people make peace with abusive family members after they were dead, but that does not happen in every case. It is important to honor those relatives you want in your life. While you may or may not choose to pray for the others, they need not be honored on a regular basis. If you don't know any names to call, that's fine. Simply call to the ancestors of your maternal line, the ancestors of your paternal line. It may be that you will learn their names in time.

When you have talked to them for a time, offer them food and drink: rice, bread, beer, wine, coffee, sweets, and even full dinners are appropriate. I usually set out a glass of wine or cup of coffee and a bit of bread or coffee cake for weekly offerings. On birth and death anniversaries, special holidays, or if I have received their aid in a very special way, I will offer more elaborate fare. Juice and water may be offered in lieu of wine and beer. I usually leave the food sitting out, but after a few hours it may be discarded. Tobacco, flowers, and incense are also appropriate offerings; in fact, you may offer anything that you personally feel called to give. Talk to your ancestors, tell them about yourself, your dreams, you goals. Tell them that you would like them to be a part of your life now. Understand that if you have not done this before, it may take time to develop a relationship—just like with any other relationship. Invite them to communicate with you, and indicate your commitment to getting to know them.

Once you feel that you have said all you wish to say, make your offerings. Thank them for their presence and for being there in your life. Thank the Goddess that you initially called for aid, and then end the ritual. Honoring the dead in such a fashion is not a one-time occurrence. It is a process of developing a very conscious awareness of our connection to the ancestors. This is something that you should commit to doing on a regular basis: weekly or at least monthly, if you really want to reap the benefits that having a strong relationship with the dead can bring. If you are able to do it, light a candle and put it on the altar, allowing it to burn out. (I often put glass-encased candles in large containers of water on my altar; that way I feel comfortable leaving them burning when I am away.) Pay attention to your dreams for the first few nights after your offerings. I have found that the dead often choose to communicate in dreams.

In addition to honoring the dead, we also honor the spirits of the land around us. The Norse word for these beings is *Vaettir* (singular, *Vaet*[9]), and they are responsible for maintaining harmony in the natural world. This term may also be used to refer to the various non-human beings that may inhabit a house or dwelling. There are some who are beneficial to humankind and others who just want to be left alone. Every stone, tree, and blade of grass has Vaettir attached to it. Any damage done to the natural world directly affects and often harms the indigenous Vaettir. As our relationship with them is, in many respects, symbiotic, they may be honored the same way as the ancestors, with a bit of beer or milk and honey, bread, and butter set out prior to any rite. Taking care to recycle and even committing an hour or so a week to picking up garbage at a local park or beach is also a nice way of honoring Vaettir.

Humanity exists in a balance between the world of the dead and the natural world. It is a balance of respect and mindfulness that each living person is charged to maintain. Consciously honoring one's ancestors; honoring the Vaettir; and living rightly, courageously, and with devotion are all means of doing just that.

Chapter 6

Heathen Ethics and Values

Being Heathen is more than just honoring the Norse Gods and Goddesses. To truly be Heathen means living one's life in a particular way, adhering to a specific set of values, and following a particular code of ethics. Where that code of ethics is lacking, so is true Heathenry. The values of the Germanic warband—honor, loyalty, forthrightness, and courage—are greatly prized; cowardice and unconditional pacifism are condemned. It is this warrior sensibility that creates the greatest gulf between Heathenry and Neo-Paganism. Within Heathenry, warriorship is not a mental or theoretical pursuit. Many Heathens own weapons (and know how to use them), choose to serve in the military, excel at hunting and the study of the martial arts, and find numerous other ways to develop in themselves a warrior's sensibilities. Willingness and readiness to defend oneself and one's family are of paramount importance to the average Heathen. While not every Heathen would define him or herself as a warrior, the virtues of honor, integrity, and bold action are valued by all.

This code of ethics is not based on Judeo-Christian mores, nor does it stem from 20th-century attitudes. It is a code of behavior drawn from the tribal structure, drawn from the cultural awareness from which celebration of the Germanic Gods evolved. It can be very difficult for a newcomer to the religion, at first, for this very reason. Developing an understanding of Heathen ethics, learning to embody them, and turning one's back on the values instilled in a non-Heathen childhood is an ongoing challenge. One way to do this is to consciously seek out opportunities to hone these newfound values and to engage in pursuits that enhance, rather than diminish, such Heathen consciousness. Being surrounded by good Heathen folk and seeking their counsel is also a useful endeavor. Developing and striving to live by this code of ethics is something that Heathens do to better serve their communities and their ancestors and to better honor the Gods. Simply choosing to address conflict directly, intelligently, and honestly rather than fleeing or avoiding is a good step in the right direction. It goes without saying that this does not mean meeting every conflict with fisticuffs or violent action. There are times when that is indeed the appropriate response, but that is hardly the case in the majority is situations. Most Heathens are peaceful, family-oriented folk. Violence would be considered appropriate only in the case of injury or threat to oneself or one's family.

The most commonly found moral axiom is called the Nine Noble Virtues. Though never directly found in any piece of Heathen lore, these virtues are culled from the "Havamal"[1] and reflect, in brief, the important values of Heathenry. The Nine Noble Virtues are not static ideals, but rather constantly evolving goals toward which we must always strive.

The Nine Noble Virtues (NNV) are as follows:

1. Courage.
2. Discipline.
3. Fidelity.
4. Honor.
5. Hospitality.
6. Industriousness.
7. Perseverance.
8. Self-Reliance.
9. Truth.

Now let's break these down for further study.

- **Courage:** Courage is the brother to fear. There is no courage that doesn't rise from terror. It is knowing when to speak and when to remain silent and having the will to act, despite difficulty or overwhelming fear. It means facing darkness, and it is the first step in learning to live by one's convictions.
- **Discipline:** Ah, what a bad word this has become in modern society! It is key to deepening one's commitment and relationship to the Gods. It is the first and most important building block in the foundation of an honorable life. It goes hand in hand with the virtue of perseverance and, as a whetstone hones a finely crafted blade, so does discipline hone the spirit, stripping away all that is not spiritually healthy. Discipline is a gift that we give to ourselves allowing us to succeed in every aspect of life.
- **Fidelity:** Developing one's relationship with the Gods is akin to falling in love—a passionate, all-consuming love affair. Fidelity is the long-term commitment, not only to the Gods but to the Kindred and tribe that walks the path with you and to the ethics which, as a Heathen, you have chosen to live by. It is a strength that gives one the ability to forbear and means not turning back when the path becomes difficult. Another word might be *loyalty*.
- **Honor:** This is the most difficult of all the virtues to describe. It defines the condition of one's spirit and, in many ways, is the accumulation of all the other virtues lived out and lived well. It is a matter of not compromising in one's relationship *or* service to Deity, no matter how difficult or trying that may, at times, become. It is consciously and willingly tearing away the comfort zone that we place between ourselves and the Gods and standing vulnerable yet strong in purpose. It means doing what is right, even when it is difficult or might bring uncomfortable consequences. Honor is living one's duty.
- **Hospitality:** This is a virtue that impacts many diverse elements of our lives. It is giving back and not only being courteous, but acknowledging Kindred as kin. It means approaching others in the spirit of "right good will." "Right good will" means you accept that those who approach you within the community are doing so honorably and without any hidden agenda or malicious intent. It gives the benefit of

the doubt that all are adhering to the same ethics and values. It is a very important concept and is what underlies the structure of the web of oaths within Theodish society. It means that we are all acting with each other's good in mind. The virtue of hospitality also involves acting honorably and with generosity. Hospitality entails one's responsibility to the world around you, including being aware of where you can make a difference. It means being willing to reach out to help the least of one's Kindred.

- **Industriousness:** Constantly striving to develop one's gifts and talents and sharing those gifts with one's Kindred, as well as using them to make an impact on the non-Kindred world at large, is part and parcel of this virtue. It entails accepting the responsibility to do your life's work as the Gods define it. It is also the responsibility to be productive with your knowledge. More to the point, it's taking pride in doing the smallest task well, for every act should be a prayer and a celebration of everything that makes one Heathen.
- **Perseverance:** Has to do with developing one's will and fortitude. It means grasping each difficulty, each failure, each fear, and each pain as a gift, blessing, challenge, and opportunity to grow stronger, wiser, and closer to the Gods. It means not giving up and keeping to your goals, and keeping the Gods, one's kin, and thew always in mind and central to your life. It goes hand in hand with discipline and, on the most mundane of levels, means working to develop healthy habits of spirituality.
- **Self-Reliance:** Ridding oneself of any unconscious motivations, tearing down blockages of ego, and moving past the codependency and self-pity that we, as a society, have been taught. It means taking responsibility not only for one's actions and their consequences but also for claiming one's active place as part of the Kindred. It means not going to the Gods only for what we can get.
- **Truth:** More than simply speaking or doing no falsehood, it means having the courage to walk honorably, despite the difficulties or discomforts. It means facing the challenges that will inevitably emerge as we cast off unneeded facades in the course of our spiritual journey and growing awareness of what it means to live in thew.

A good way to develop an understanding of these virtues is to take some time to define them for yourself—to elaborate on what they mean to you personally and how you manifest them in your daily life. Where do you fall short? Where and how can you improve? What special talents and gifts do you bring to your Gods and your community?

There is a saying within Heathenry: "We are our deeds."[2] This essentially defines Heathen ethics better than anything else. It is the quality of one's deeds and the spirit in which they are performed that either strengthens or weakens the individual and his or her community. Heathen values are not based on a concept of sin and redemption, but of right action and divine order. There is that which enhances one's wyrd, one's tribe, and one's own life and luck to the benefit of all—and that which does not. And for every act which does not, there are consequences.

In addition to the Nine Noble Virtues, there are also the "Twelve Ætheling Thews."[3] Some of these are contained within the Nine Noble Virtues, but others expand upon and complement them. Because this particular code of ethics evolved within the Anglo-Saxon Heathen community, the name for each virtue is in Old English.

The Twelve Ætheling Thews are:

1. Besignes—Industriousness.
2. Efnes—Equality and equal justice for everyone, regardless of gender, race, social standing, etc.
3. Ellen—Courage.
4. Geférscipe—This is perhaps the essence of tribalism: putting the good and needs of the community above one's self and utilizing one's own unique talents to enhance the luck of the tribe as a whole.
5. Giefu—Generosity.
6. Giestlíðness—Hospitality.
7. Metgung—Moderation and self-control. Though it's never stated explicitly, moderation is stressed throughout the "Havamal," as the primary attribute of an honorable person.

8. Selfdóm—Nurturing one's individual talents, being true to oneself.
9. Sóð—Truth and honesty.
10. Stedefæstnes—Steadfastness.
11. Tréowð—Loyalty, troth.
12. Wísdóm—Wisdom.

(This list of virtues is covered in greater depth by Eric Wodening in his book *We Are Our Deeds* and by Swain Wodening in *Hammer of the Gods*.)

Additionally, underlying the ethics and values of Heathen society is the concept of "frith." Many folk define frith as "peace," but that is not quite accurate. A far better translation of the term would be "right order."[4] Adherence to frith, mindfulness of its boundaries, was the very thing which ensured a cohesive, harmonious, well-functioning community. It kept discord at a minimum and, at the very least, provided means by which grievances could be addressed. Frith is the foundation of thew. A frithstead is a place wherein no violence or ill action may be committed, for to do so not only damages one's luck, but may lead to various community penalties, from being forced to pay a "shild," or debt of honor, to outcasting from the community. The fact that many Goddesses, especially Frigga, were referred to as "Frith-weavers" underscores its importance in Heathen culture.

In addition to the virtues mentioned, many other qualities are valued within Heathen society, including wisdom, eloquence, compassion, and freedom of conscience. All of these attributes are considered necessary building blocks of civilized Heathen culture. Ultimately, however, each person is responsible for his or her orlog, responsible for ensuring that he or she is remembered with honor.

Chapter 7

The Basic Blót

All denominations of Heathenry share one thing in common: the blót. Taken from an Old Norse word for "sacrifice," the word *blót* (pronounced to rhyme with *boat*) is used by modern Heathens to indicate a generic Heathen ritual. Indeed, it forms the foundation for all of Heathen worship, and many important tenets of practice and faith can be found in this relatively simple rite. The word *blót* was originally thought to translate as "to strengthen" (the Gods).[1] Given the reciprocal obligations of gift-giving among the Norse, it would follow that strengthening the Gods led to a strengthening of one's personal health, wealth, luck, and well-being, as well as that of one's kin.

One of the most thorough descriptions of a blót can be found in Snorri Sturluson's *Heimskringla*:

> It was an old custom, that when there was to be sacrifice all the bondes should come to the spot where the temple stood and bring with them all that they required while the festival of the sacrifice lasted. To this festival all the men brought ale with them; and all kinds of cattle, as well as horses, were slaughtered, and all the blood that came from them was called "hlaut", and the vessels in which it was collected were called hlaut-vessels. Hlaut-staves were made, like sprinkling brushes, with which the whole of the

> altars and the temple walls, both outside and inside, were sprinkled over, and also the people were sprinkled with the blood; but the flesh was boiled into savoury meat for those present. The fire was in the middle of the floor of the temple, and over it hung the kettles, and the full goblets were handed across the fire; and he who made the feast, and was a chief, blessed the full goblets, and all the meat of the sacrifice. And first Odin's goblet was emptied for victory and power to his king; thereafter, Niord's and Freyja's goblets for peace and a good season. Then it was the custom of many to empty the brage-goblet[2]; and then the guests emptied a goblet to the memory of departed friends, called the remembrance goblet.[3]

The format of standard rituals within modern Heathenry is largely drawn from descriptions such as this one found in the Icelandic Sagas and other first- and secondhand sources of the time. The motivation behind them comes from the Havamal and the exhortations toward gift-giving and a sharing of wealth amongst the tribe found there. As we are given many good things by the Gods, so the blót provides an opportunity for us to show our gratitude and to give something back. The purpose of the blót is actually twofold: not only does it provide an opportunity for communion with the Gods, but it is also a "folk-binding" ritual. In other words, it brings folk together in celebration and friendship, it increases the feeling of kinship amongst participants, and it strengthens the bonds of hospitality. These things are very important in the minds of modern Heathens.

At its core, the blót is about sacrifice. The concept of sacrifice is one of the integral tenets of Heathenry. It is enshrined in our lore where we are called to remember Odin hanging on the Tree, in nine nights of agony, in exchange for the runes. It is part and parcel of frith where the exchange of gifts, food, drink, and hospitality creates a bond of reciprocity between giver and receiver. It is this, perhaps more than any other practice, ethic, or virtue, that sets Heathenry apart from Neo-Paganism: we commune with our Gods (in part) through an established system of gift-giving. Through this, we receive blessings in return, yet nurture our own strength and self-reliance. The "Havamal" exhorts us to go often to our friends' homes and to exchange gifts regularly. By doing so, a bond of affection and obligation is established. The blót provides the Heathen with the opportunity for just such an exchange with the Gods. Far from being self-serving bribery, it is a well-established ancient tradition wherein two parties enter into a web of duty, obligation, and—yes—affection, thereby also entering into a pact of frith.[4] The blót was and is a way of inviting the Gods to participate in the household and community, to come and enter and be welcomed as honored guests with all that, to the Heathen mind, this entails.

As explained previosuly, through the Sagas we do have surviving accounts of how a blót was performed. Let's examine the various parts of this ritual.

- Folk gather.

  Congregants come together at a designated time and place to honor the Gods. Folk may bring wine, food, and other offerings. If there is to be a feast, the preparations would take place at this time or slightly before.

- The space is hallowed.

  Once everyone is gathered and it is time for the rite to begin, the officiant hallows the space. Depending on one's denomination, this may be done by a sacred chant calling upon the protective power of the God Thor to banish all evil. Or it may be done by a mini-rite called a "Hammer Hallowing," which invokes the power of Thor's hammer to protect the sacred area. For one new to the religion or one performing a blót by him- or herself, carrying a candle around the ritual space and sincerely asking Thor to hallow and bless the space is perfectly acceptable and efficient.

- The offerings (usually wine and food) are blessed. Folk may be sprinkled with wine in lieu of the sacrificial blood mentioned in the sagas.

  The officiant blesses the offerings and the feast. An evergreen sprig is dipped in the offering wine and the congregants are sprinkled with the wine. Some may choose to omit this part of the rite if there is no attendant feast.

- The Gods are called in invocation and prayer.

  The officiant hails the Gods and Goddesses. There is no limit to how many Deities may be called, but usually blóts are either Deity specific (such as a Woden blót, Frigga blót, etc.) or for some special occasion (baby blessing, holy day, etc.). One would not hail every single God and Goddess in the span of one blót.

- A horn, symbolizing the Well of memory and fate, is passed around the gathered folk. People may offer prayers to the Gods, hail their ancestors, or boast of their own deeds.

  Sometimes the horn will just be passed person to person; sometimes a woman of high regard and status within the group will carry the horn from person to person. The first time the horn is carried around, each person raises the horn and offers a prayer to a God or Goddess.

  The second time the horn is passed, each person may hail an ancestor. The third time, one may boast of deeds that have been accomplished. This threefold action is later expanded into the most sacred of all Heathen rituals: Symbel.

- If the rite includes a feast, it takes place at this point. Some of the food and drink is set aside for Vaettir (land spirits, analogous to the Japanese *kami*), ancestors, and Gods.

  The officiant offers alcohol and part of the feast to the Gods, Vaettir and ancestors, placing it before the altar or pouring it out in a special bowl used only for ritual (a blessing bowl). The remainder of the feast is then shared amongst the participants. If there is no feast, wine is offered to the Gods, ancestors, and Vaettir with accompanying thanks.

- Thanks are offered to the Gods, and the rite is adjourned.

  The officiant gives thanks to the Gods and ancestors, and the remains of the wine, mead, or beer is poured out in offering. A prayer may be said in closing. I personally like to sing the Valkyrie's prayer from the "Sigdrifumal" in the *Poetic Edda*:

  Hail to the Day, and Day's sons.
  Hail to Night and Her daughters.

With loving eyes, look upon us here
And bring victory.
Hail to the Gods,
Hail to the Goddesses,
Hail to the mighty, fecund earth.
Eloquence, wisdom, and native wit
Bestow on your children here.
And healing hands while we live.[5]

- At this point, the rite is closed, and folk may mingle as they wish.

In the past, before Christianity spread across Europe, the average blót would generally have involved some sort of animal sacrifice. It was a communal feast. In some denominations of Heathenry, particularly Tribalist or Theodish groups, the word *blót* refers *only* to rites in which animal sacrifice takes place. In such rites, the animal, usually a swine or goat, is honored and treated with great solemnity. During the blót, the space is hallowed with a sacred song, the Gods are invoked, a horn is passed amongst all participants, and then the animal is sacrificed cleanly and quickly. It is done in as painless a manner as possible, usually with a blade, sometimes with a rifle. If the animal suffers in any way, it is a hideously bad omen. The blood of the animal is captured in the blót bowl and sprinkled on the attending participants, in an act of blessing. The ritual is then concluded. At this point, the animal is cleaned, cooked, and later served as part of a sacred feast. Every part of the animal must be eaten or consigned to a sacred fire as an offering to the Gods. Nothing is wasted. Such sacrifice is done only at very special occasions, such as Yule or Midsummer, and affects the luck of the entire tribe. Generic rituals, done to honor the Gods but without sacrifice, are called *fainings*.

The concept of sharing food as a means of communing with the Gods did not originate with Christianity. Some form of this ritual may be found in nearly every religion from Mithraism to Celtic worship to Judaism to the religions of the Far East, and nearly all cultures and religions before Christianity had a custom of offering food to both the dead and to the Gods. It is a very potent act. Food symbolizes health, wealth, and nourishment. It is abundance and caring. By entering into sacred space and sharing these things, even in symbolic fashion, with our Gods, we are opening ourselves to being nourished by the Gods just as much as we are celebrating the blessings the Gods have given. When a blót involves the sacrifice of an animal and communal feast, it is commonly called *husel*, a word that early English Christians adopted for their own rite of communion.

Numerous things, including animals, might be sacrificed in the course of husels of old, and this holds true today. Certain animals tended to be associated with certain Deities (for example, boars for Freyr, horses for Odin, and goats for Thor), and making such a sacrifice, which in most cases inevitably culminated in a feast, was yet another way of bringing the community together and of celebrating kinship and frith. (Animal sacrifice is only practiced by a small minority of modern Heathens. It's far more common to simply cook up a roast purchased at the local supermarket.) Of course other items might be offered as well. It is important to understand that, at its root, the word *sacrifice* means "to make sacred." It is not a matter of sacrificing for the sake of sacrifice alone, but of sacrificing in order to draw closer to the Gods—very much like giving a gift to a loved one. By extending that metaphorical hand in welcome to the Gods, by gift-giving and throwing open the doors of our homes, hearts, and consciousness, we sanctify, we make sacred not only the dwelling in which we celebrate, but ourselves and that which is being offered as well. Therefore, the offering need not be an animal. Modern Heathens may offer anything from flowers to beer to food to volunteer work. It is the willingness to enter into a relationship with the Gods that is important.

Eric Wodening, in his article "Knowest How to Blót," points out that the Old English word *bletsian* ("to bless") may be related etymologically to the Norse word *blót*. Both have connotations of "to bless with blood." In the description of a blót found in "Hákonar Saga goða," of the *Heimskringla* (quoted previously), the gathered folk are sprinkled with sacrificial blood. This hallowing with blood is highly potent symbolically. Our connection to our folk, our kin, and our ancestors is a connection forged not only in spirit, but in blood. The Hamingja[6] is passed on through the blood. And we are said to be blood-kin to the Gods, descended from and tutored by Them. The Eddic poem "Rigsthula" tells the story of how the God Heimdall wandered, disguised, amongst humanity, fathering children on every woman who showed him hospitality. Some scholars believe that this may have actually been Odin, not Heimdall, for it is well attested to in the lore that Odin likes the ladies; however, modern Heathens generally agree that humanity is the kin of Heimdall. This ritualized sprinkling with blood can be seen as a vivid reminder of that sacred connection. It is a call to arms, urging us to live up to all that entails, not only in our relationship with our Gods but in our relationship with each other and our communities.

This hallowing then, is a hallowing and awakening of memory, ancestral memory, and spiritual duty. The same could be said for lifting the horn, for though not every blót will include an animal sacrifice and feast, every blót should include that mindful awareness that each of us stands as an ongoing link in a chain of ancestors stretching back to the beginning. We are the ancestors upon whose shoulders those who follow us will stand. It is that mindfulness—that connection with the Gods and our honored dead—that creates the blót. All else, however potent a symbol, is merely a reminder of that essential fact.

In our Judeo-Christian culture, hallowing and sacrifice bring to mind connotations of pious abstention, but the reality among the Heathen cultures of old was far different. For us, sacrifice is a means of claiming personal power, of opening ourselves to wisdom and knowledge, and of drawing close to the Gods Who are our friends and loved Ones. And being the pragmatic folk that so many Heathens are, there is a certain quid pro quo about the whole thing: I will do this or give this, and it will open up the possibility of receiving something in return. Moreover, it's about remembering where we come from. Everything we have, in some way, comes from the Gods—even the breath that gives our bodies life. It's only proper to remember and honor that. At it's basest level, it's about respect, courtesy, and gratitude. It is a celebration of our kinship with the Gods.

Personal Faining

Following is a sample of how I do personal faining. This is a basic outline, and it's important to remember that any sacred ritual needs to leave room for fluidity of experience. Before the rite begins, I cleanse the room and set up an altar. Like many Heathen clergy, I maintain an altar all the time, but before any rite, I may change its design and make it more Deity-specific. An altar is a living thing, reflecting the heart of one's spiritual practice. It should never be left neglected or in disrepair. Because ritual should speak to all the senses—sight, smell, sound, and feeling—and by doing so, carry folks into the realm of the sacred, opening them to a palpable sense of the holy, I will often have candles on the altar and use incense to cleanse the room and create a certain ambiance.

Before every ritual or blót, the ritual room is purified both by being physically cleaned and smudged with *recels* (incense). Because the Goddess Frigga is specifically associated with a strong, hallowed home, I have created an incense that is dedicated to Her and Her 12 handmaidens—all powerful Goddesses in Their own right.

Purification and Protection Incense

Start with 7 Tablespoons of white sandalwood.

For Frigga, the Allmother,
add: 1 Tablespoon of rosemary.

For Fulla, Her sister and most cherished companion,
add: 1 Tablespoon of mistletoe.

For Saga, Goddess of lore, history and sacred stories,
add: 1 Tablespoon of hyssop.

For Eir, the Divine Physician,
add: 1 Tablespoon of mullein.

For Var, Who hears all sacred vows,
add: 1 Tablespoon of mint.

For Hlin, Who Defends and protects,
add: 1 Tablespoon of ash.

For Vor, Who knows all secrets,
add: 1 Tablespoon of mugwort.

For Sjofn, Who inclines the heart to love,
add: 1 Tablespoon of linden.

For Lofn, Who helps loved ones come together against all opposition,
add: 1 Tablespoon of vetivert.

For Gefion, Goddess of abundance,
add: 1 Tablespoon of juniper.

For Gná, Frigga's speedy messenger,
add: 1 Tablespoon of comfrey.

For Syn, Who wards and shields,
add: 1 Tablespoon of alkanet.

For Snotra, Goddess of graciousness and frith,
add: 1 Tablespoon of elder.

Blend all of herbs together thoroughly and store the mixture in an airtight jar. This is an excellent cleansing and purification incense. I personally like to cleanse my ritual room before and after any rite, particularly if guests attended. It's good metaphysical hygiene. This incense is burned over small charcoal pieces that can be purchased at any metaphysical or occult supply store.

If there is to be a feast, I make all the necessary preparations a couple of hours before the rite. Several bottles of mead and at least one bottle of aquavit are uncorked and set before the altar.

I. Hallowing

I use Thorsson's Hammer Hallowing[7] in Old Norse or the Ealdriht Weonde[8] song in Old English. I love the resonance of the languages. One might just as easily light two candles on the altar and ask Thor to bless and ward the room.

II. Prayer to the Ancestors and Offering to the Vaettir

I hail my honored dead, mothers and fathers generations back.
I hail your triumphs and honor your sorrows.
I remember you and will speak your names with welcome in my home. For I am here, strong and whole and proud

because of your struggles and sacrifices. I carry your blood in my veins and your courage in my heart. [*Name specific ancestors*], I remember you and hail you here tonight. [*Pour out wine or mead in offering.*] I offer this to you in remembrance.

[*Pour out more wine.*] I offer this to the Vaettir and ask that you lend your blessings to this rite that we are about to perform. Hail and welcome.

III. Prayer to Odin

Allfather, I ask for Your blessings.
Breathe into me, Oh God of gainful council.
Nourish me, Wish-Giver, that I might know You more fully and well.
Remove any blockages that might keep me from being truly open to Your presence.
I hail You, God of wisdom, cunning, and inspiration.
Wondrous Healer, Nourisher, Welcome One,
Be welcome in my life, my home, my heart.
Master of the Tree, I sacrifice to You
My fears, my doubt, my hesitation.
Breathe into me. Open me, Wisest Lord.
I will seek You with the fervor with which You sought the runes.
Be my mead, be my joy, be the prize at the end of my seeking.
Hail, Allfather, Woden, Wondrous Lord.[9]

[At this point, aquavit, which I personally associate with Odin, is tasted and poured out in the blessing bowl for Him.]

IV. Faining

The horn is filled with mead (or wine) and passed around to each person in the group several times. The first time, Odin is honored. After that, other Gods, Goddesses, and (finally) individual ancestors may be hailed. Sometimes folks may choose to tell stories about specific ancestors or relate experiences with the Gods that moved them deeply. If one does not own a drinking horn, a chalice may be used instead.

V. Feasting

The food is brought out, blessed in the name of Frigga and Odin, and shared among the participants, after first offering sizeable portions to Odin, the Vaettir, and ancestors.

VI. Thanksgiving

Odin may be thanked extempore, the Vaettir and ancestors are thanked, and any remaining alcohol is given to them. The altar candles are blown out, the rite ended, and participants dispersed. The contents of the blessing bowl should be poured out in the garden or, for city dwellers, outside. (It can be poured down the sink in a pinch, but personally, I feel this lacks finesse.)

After everyone is gone, the ritual room should again be smudged and purified with herbs.

That is all there is to the entire faining process. This basic format can be expanded upon as one gains more confidence and ritual technique. Of course, minor variations may be encountered from Kindred to Kindred, but this is essentially it. The important thing is to enter into the rite with mindfulness, respect, devotion, and a conscious desire to honor the Gods. As a rite, blót or faining may stand alone or as part of a larger celebration. It is the foundational building block of Heathen worship.

Chapter 8

Symbel

The holiest and most significant of Heathen rites is called Symbel. Symbel is essentially a rite of offering and libation. Alcohol (or a suitable nonalcoholic substance, if desired) is passed around and consumed by the attendees, while honoring the Gods and calling to mind the luck and deeds of the gathered folk. Symbel serves many purposes: it is a folk-binding ritual, it reinforces the duties and worth of every attendee, and it celebrates Heathen values and heroic culture. In many respects, this ritual is the quintessential microcosm of tribal unity. Its importance in Heathen liturgy and communion cannot be overestimated. So integral was Symbel to Germanic culture, that accounts were even incorporated into Christian texts such as the *The Heliand: The Saxon Gospel*. Here, we find the Last Supper referred to as "the last meadhall feast with the warrior-companions," and the atmosphere of the wedding of Canaan is described in terms that directly hearken back to the atmosphere of the meadhall: "The conviviality of the earls in the drinking hall was a beautiful sight, and the men on the benches had received a very high level of bliss...."[1]

Obviously the rite of Symbel continued to hold power over even the Christian mind well after the initial conversion. In many respects, it was a unifying thread between Heathen society and that which followed it.

Much like certain Gods and Goddesses who later became revered as Christian saints,[2] this ritual was not easily gotten rid of. It defined Germanic and Scandinavian society.

There are four primary parts to a good Symbel, each of which will be discussed:

1. Hallowing.
2. The Fulls.
3. Beots and gielps.
4. Gift-giving.

Symbel is a ritual of mindfulness in both speech and action. Each sacred action serves to strengthen the unity and interconnected luck between all participants. It is important to remember that, to the Heathen mind, luck is part of the soul, a living thing that may be nourished and strengthened by mindful care or damaged by careless speech, ill-conceived actions, and cowardly nonaction. In Symbel, Heathens are called to remember those past deeds, which strengthened their luck and brought might to the group, and they are called to rise above those deeds that may have been less shining. It is an opportunity to commit oneself to personal betterment.

Symbel is both a sacred rite and a celebration of community and its structure. The atmosphere is at once both one of joy and awe. Through mindful speech and ritualized gift-giving, Symbel calls to mind the strength and cohesiveness of the community, setting each and every person not only in the active flow of wyrd, but bringing them into conscious alignment with the wisdom and might of their collective ancestral line. This rite unites the community, weaving bonds of loyalty and friendship amongst the gathered folk, and consciously sets forth their collective deeds in the eyes of the Gods. Symbel is, above all else, a ritual of fate-weaving. It is a celebration of frith, community, and commitment to future evolution. Additionally, the structured nature of Symbel affirms both social values and tribal hierarchy, "reaffirming the identify of the group and of the individuals within that group."[3] Though it bears some cursory resemblance to blót and faining in its initial structure, it is far more complex and tightly ordered.

Examples of Symbel permeate the surviving lore, giving modern practitioners a fairly clear idea of how the rite was practiced in pre-Christian Northern Europe. We find examples not only amongst the Anglo-Saxon, but in Scandinavian and Norse texts, as well. The most well-known and clear-cut example of Symbel in the lore occurs in *Beowulf*:

> *Then a bench was cleared, room made in the hall*
> *for the gathered warriors, standing in a troop;*
> *the courageous men, took their seats,*
> *proud in their strength; a thane did his office,*
> *carried in his hands the gold ale-flagons,*
> *poured bright mead. At times the scop sang,*
> *bright-voiced in Heorot; there was joy of warriors....*

Here we see that Symbel was held inside, in the feasting hall, after the primary feast. We see that the ritual incorporated both praise songs and sacred speech. The nobility of the rite is emphasized, as well as its importance to the gathered warriors. Later on, we are given even greater insight into the nature of this ritual:

> *The noble lady gave the first cup,*
> *filled to the brim, to the king of the Danes,*
> *bade him rejoice in this mead-serving,*
> *beloved by his people, he took it happily,*
> *victory-famed king, the hall-cup and feast.*
> *The lady of the Helmings walked through the hall,*
> *offered the jeweled cup to veterans and youths,*
> *until the time came that courteous queen,*
> *splendid in rings, excellent in virtues,*
> *came to Beowulf, brought him the mead.*
> *She greeted him well, gave thanks to God,*
> *wise in her words, that her wish came to pass,*
> *that she might expect help against crimes*
> *from any man. He accepted the cup,*
> *battle-fierce warrior, from Wealhtheow's hand,*
> *Then made a speech, eager for combat..."*[4]

This excerpt illustrates several important parts of a traditional Symbel—most notably, the important role women play in structuring the ritual and maintaining a sense of the sacred.[5] We also see that Symbel included mighty boasts. In fact, though there may be minor variations from Kindred to Kindred, the basic outline of a Symbel may be broken down into the following parts:

- **Hallowing.**

  In many cases, the rite begins with a ritual blessing, either the Hammer Hallowing or the Weonde. In other cases, this is forgone in favor of a simple declaration that Symbel has now begun. Over and above anything else, the defining aspect of Symbel is that it is a ritual of mindful, sacred speech. What is said becomes active fate. What is spoken directly impacts the luck of the individual, as well as of the tribe as a whole. Verbally intoning that Symbel has begun can be as effective as any type of hallowing. Generally, folk are seated according to their position or rank within the Kindred or tribe before this hallowing takes place. At this time, the host (or hostess) may also give a brief introductory speech, stating the purpose of the gathering, praising the group's accomplishments, expressing joy at being united with everyone again, or otherwise speaking in a manner that eloquently sets the mood and tone of the ritual to come.

- **The *valkyrie* (Old Norse) or *ealu bora* (Old English) pours the beverage of choice into the ritual horn. She first offers the horn to the host or hostess and later carries it around to the assembled guests hailing them with wise words and offering them a draught.**

  Several important facets of this particular part of the rite are worth noting here. In many respects, the *ealu bora* is the most important person in the entire Symbel. In traditional Heathenry, this role is *always* fulfilled by a woman. At first, this may seem like a gender-bias that casts the woman in a subservient role, but nothing could be further from the truth. Germanic culture has always regarded women as being innately holy. Women were believed to have a special connection to the numinous, and many were said to possess the gift of prophecy. As early as 98 C.E., Tacitus records, with some surprise, the high regard in which the Germanic tribes held their women, particularly esteemed seeresses such as the renowned Veleda, who foretold the defeat of the Roman legions.[6] Furthermore, women were connected to fate and the structuring of wyrd in a way that no man could hope to be.

In traditional Germanic culture, one of the primary feminine arts was that of spinning and weaving. Indeed, this was absolutely necessary to the smooth running of a household. There were no Wal-Marts or superstores from which to buy one's clothing. Everything was made by hand at home, usually under the auspices of the lady of the house, if not by her own hand. The lady would be responsible for overseeing the manufacture of everything needed to adequately clothe and run the household. The ancient Heathens early on recognized a symbolic parallel between the mortal arts of spinning and weaving and the actions of the Nornir who spun and wove layers of fate. "Weaving and spinning of textiles could easily become a microcosm for the greater macrocosm of weaving the web of existence."[7] This connects women indisputably to the power of the Nornir, and it is as Their representative that a woman presides over Symbel. As the Nornir weave strands of fate, so women weave frith during Symbel, ensuring that the oaths and boasts are layered properly into the tribal orlog. The ealu bora, deciding the order in which the horn is passed from person to person, also reinforces social structure and tribal hierarchy. It is the wisdom and power of the woman that makes the Symbel a holy rite.

What we see in Symbel is a balanced union of "worth" and "frith"—might and right order. In many orthodox denominations of Heathenry, men are said to predominantly manifest worth, and women, frith. This does not mean that a man cannot be a peace-weaver or a woman manifest sacred might, but we are discussing overall sacred roles patterned largely after the Allfather and Allmother, both of Whom are mighty in Their Own rights. Worth and frith are easily likened to chaos and order. Both serve necessary purposes but they must go hand in hand for healthy growth and evolution to occur. Allow one to rule or reign out of control and disharmony, and disaster may ensue. It is the same in Symbel. Because one of the main actions during Symbel is the taking of oaths and the boasting of honorable deeds over the horn (all acts of worth), it is all the more necessary to have the rite ordered by one who embodies frith. To quote Dan O'Halloran, Aetheling Lord of Normanni Reiks in New York:

> *During blót/Symbel, a theodsman*[8] *may never exchange a horn man to man—it must ALWAYS be grounded by a frithy presence (a female). The metaphysical explanation is quite simple: men in general and boasting in particular are "worthy" acts. Worth attracts wights and builds Maegen; unchecked this leads to recklessness of the tongue, bragging (not in the positive sense), the attraction of woeful wights, and impure beoting. When worth dominates frith, it places the rite out of spiritual balance. Women ground and bring frith to the horn, thus setting aright the balance with the Well and preventing an accumulation of over-worthy Maegen. It is the complimentary give and take that makes Symbel productive.*[9]

A word should be said about the predominance of alcohol in Heathen rituals. The passing of a horn is a highly symbolic act. The horn represents the Well of Wyrd, Urðabrunnr, into which all fate and memory eventually flow. The waters of this Well nourish the World Tree, and both the Well and the Tree are tended by Urð, the Norn of all that has been and all that will become. During Symbel, in sacred thought, the Well and the horn become one. This is why words spoken over the horn during this rite create strands of fate that are then ordered into the collective wyrd. It is precisely this understanding that makes Symbel a fate-weaving rite.

The use of alcohol, generally mead, is representative of Oðroerir, the mead of poetry, eloquence, and ecstatic inspiration. Verbal eloquence and poetic skill were highly prized among the Germanic and Scandinavian peoples. Poets were regarded with an almost sacred reverence. Moreover, "just as all mead in ritual settings echoes the mead of poetry gained by Oðinn, there is a special efficacious quality to all things spoken over the cup, and so the women who served in this function signified the frith-weaving of community bonds."[10] Additionally, the liquid in the horn symbolizes the healing waters of

Urðabrunnr. Of course, nonalcoholic beverages may also be used, and many Kindreds, particularly those in which there are folk in recovery, choose to have two horns carried by the valkyrie: one with mead or wine and another with juice. If it is the best that can be offered, there is nothing inherently wrong with filling a horn with plain drinking water.

To further elaborate on the importance of women in Symbel and their inherent connection to wyrd, it should be noted that the ealu bora becomes the embodiment of Urð, and it is Urð's power which sustains the World Tree, which in turn, sustains all creation. Furthermore, even the Gods must bow to the strictures of the fate ordered by the Nornir. It is the woman (the active fate-weaver) who creates Symbel. To quote Lord Dan O'Halloran again:

> *Sitting at Symbel is an act of setting words into the Well in a metaphysical attempt to affect Wyrd and direct it. It is the feminine aspect that is "active" in this task and carries the water to the Well, sprinkling the Tree, and forcing the dynamic cycle of Wyrd to flow. It is the Woman who bares the Wyrd back and forth to the Well—which of course is ALSO the metaphysical embodiment of the feminine "frithy" part to the Tree's "worthy" masculine part.*[11]

Of course, there may be occasions where no women are present. While this is rare, it may occasionally occur. In a case like this, if Symbel cannot be postponed until a woman is able to attend, the horn should then be passed by a man who has a strong connection to one of the Goddesses. Certain denominations will still find this unacceptable and would simply not hold Symbel. Other more liberal sects do not adhere overmuch to the tradition of having women only pass the horn.

- **The Fulls.**

Before bearing the horn to anyone else, the valkyrie passes it first to the *symbelgerefa*, the host or hostess, saluting him or her with carefully thought-out words. The symbelgerefa, upon accepting the horn, makes a series of three prayers, or *fulls*, and thereby sets the tone for the entire Symbel.

The first full consists of prayers or hails to the Gods. Here, the symbelgerefa usually honors the group's (be it Kindred, Mot, or Maethel) three most popular Gods or Goddesses.

For instance, my Kindred is given to Woden primarily. The Maethel that we are part of is under Ingvi Frey's protection, and as a Kindred, we have dedicated the year's work to Eir. Therefore, at a Kindred Symbel, I would most likely hail first Woden, then Frey, and then Eir, offering a toast to each. At a Tribal Symbel, Frey would be hailed first.

Next, the symbelgerefa hails and toasts the luck, or Maegen of the gathered group. He or she may call to mention specific deeds and even speak briefly about the history of the group and everything that has passed since the last Symbel. This is not meant to be a tediously long toast, but a concise and vivid reconstruction of those actions that have had the most potent influence on the group as a whole. This is a time to call the collective Maegen into the spotlight, putting it on the table, so to speak, in full metaphorical view of the gathered folk, Gods, and Nornir.

The third full is commonly called the *bragafull* and usually consists of boasts for the group's upcoming goals and plans of action. The symbelgerefa openly discusses his or her plans for the group's upcoming season. Goals are set into motion, verbally and esoterically laid into the warp and weft of the group wyrd. This is a very important part of the ritual, for what is spoken over the horn becomes woven inexorably into being and fate and carries with it a definite obligation. Failure to fulfill oaths and boasts thus made can lead to a weakening of might and luck for everyone concerned. It is, in many ways, equivalent to spiritual *devolution*.

After the symbelgerefa has made the requisite fulls, the ealu bora carries the horn around to each person gathered, usually in order of rank. Less hierarchical Kindreds may simply pass the horn as in blót: clockwise around the gathered folk, but always to and from the hand of the valkyrie. The first round is given completely to the ancestors and is called the *Minni-horn*, or horn of memory. In later rounds, as the horn is being passed, each person may hail friends, ancestors, and kinsman.

Unlike a faining, which is specifically oriented toward Gods, Symbel is folk-oriented. Whereas a blót or faining has as its primary purpose honoring the Gods, in Symbel, the ultimate goal is binding the folk together, increasing their collective luck, and weaving new collective wyrd. While the Gods and Goddesses may certainly be hailed in the various rounds, it is just as common to hail friends, family, and the honored dead.

- **Beots and gielps.**

The horn is usually passed several times around the gathered folk. The first time, as mentioned previously, kinsman and friends are hailed. During the later rounds, one may continue to do this, or conversely, one may choose to make a beot or gielp.

A *beot* is an oath, or sacred promise, made in the presence of Gods and kin. It is often a vow to perform some deed or undertake some specific work that will bring honor to oneself and one's Kindred. For example, at the Kindred Symbel on Yule of 2003, I made a beot to complete a book of devotionals to Woden within the year. It was to be a gift to Him, and this vow was completed in July 2004.[12] As Pollington points out, calling a beot and gielp a *vow* or *boast* does not truly capture the power of uttering these ritual words.[13] They were more than just simple utterances, they were incantations of power and strength, a consciously active structuring of one's personal fate. In fact, they may be seen as a way of challenging fate and improving one's lot. One's Maegen or Hamingja may be strengthened by the fulfilling of difficult oaths. Pollington goes on to point out that the word *beot* is "derived from *bi-hat* 'calling' (*hatan* 'to call, to name')" and it is connected to the "Germanic notion of single-combat and dueling.[14]

A *gielp* is a boast of past deeds. Often this is preceded by a recitation of one's lineage and ancestry[15] and of one's own worth and place within the kin-group. It is of utmost importance not to ever exaggerate or speak falsely when making either a gielp or a beot. This is not a time for overly prideful bragging, but a time to honestly and sincerely recount those ways in which one contributed to the good of the whole. The "Havamal" states that:

"Cattle die, kinsmen die,
the self must also die,
but glory never dies,
for the man who is able to achieve it.

Cattle die, kinsmen die,
The self must also die;
I know one thing which never dies:
The reputation of each dead man."[16]

This excerpt brilliantly illustrates the warrior ethos of the arch-Heathens, one that is being resurrected today amongst modern practitioners. One's *gefrain* ("good name or reputation"), one's deeds, and the work of one's hands are of utmost importance to the modern Heathen mind. They are the measure of a man or woman, and it is this that is allowed to shine forth in Symbel. It is, in part, for this reason that Heathens oath and boast during this rite.

Every gielp or beot made is woven directly into the fabric of wyrd. They are powerful and binding both in the eyes of the Gods and in the flow of wyrd. A broken oath or a misspoken gielp can have negative repercussions for all involved—even those who only witnessed the ill-chosen words. Ensuring that no ill consequences befall the group from poorly spoken words and acting to counterbalance the force of the speaker's will is the role of the *Thyle*. The Thyle maintains the order and integrity of all words spoken within Symbel and may challenge anyone's gielps or beots without breaking the frith. In fact, in Symbel, the Thyle is instrumental in maintaining frith, which, after all, is not just harmony and peace, but right order as well. The role of the Thyle is usually maintained by the man or woman most knowledgeable in lore, tribal customs, Kindred history, and ritual structure. It is the *obligation* of the Thyle to challenge any toast, oath, or boast that is not based in honesty and integrity. The Thyle is the one person in all of Symbel who ensures that nothing untoward is laid into the communal wyrd. He or she guards and maintains the luck-weaving, thereby removing this burden from the symbelgerefa and ealu boru for the duration of the ritual.

- **Gift-giving.**

  During the third round of passing the horn, the symbelgerefa and/ or the lord/lady of the Maethel or hall may choose to bestow gifts on their gathered folk. In Anglo-Saxon and Scandinavian society, the lord was a ring-giver, the lady, a loaf-giver. They bestowed gifts and nourishment on their folk in exchange for loyalty, friendship, and service. These gifts were marks of trust and the reciprocal relationship maintained by everyone within the social hierarchy. Though in some modern Symbels everyone exchanges gifts, historically and in more traditional denominations of Heathenry, it is only those in the leadership position who bestow gifts on the gathered folk. Each gift carries with it reciprocal obligations of loyalty and friendship. The exchange strengthens bonds between folk and, like everything else in Symbel, is a highly symbolic act. Each gift is a token of esteem and honor[17] and is imbued with the luck of the group. Gifts are given to each person in order of their rank and social station.

After the third round, the horn may be passed as many more times as desired. Songs may be sung, stories told, and poems recited in place of toasts or beots or gielps. Though a solemn ritual, Symbel should not be devoid of joy and laughter. It is a celebration of everything that makes a Kindred or Maethel a community. At the end of Symbel, the remaining alcohol should be poured into a *blótorc*, or blessing bowl. The symbelgerefa formally announces that Symbel has come to an end and may choose to offer thanks to the three Gods hailed at the beginning of Symbel. After this, folk are free to disperse. Someone, either a priest or the ealu boru, takes the blessing bowl and pours its contents into the earth, in offering to the Gods and Vaettir.

Chapter 9

Personal Devotions

Spiritual opening is difficult. Often it seems equal parts grace, discipline, hard work, and sometimes the proverbial blood, sweat, and tears. It is a process that demands all the vigilance of a master warrior and the patience of a master gardener. And most frightening of all, it is a process that we ourselves seldom control or even comprehend. Opening to the ineffable presence of the Divine can be a truly terrifying thing. It strips us away from all that is safe, comfortable, and known. It challenges us to be better than we are, better than anything in our spiritually bereft world tells us to be. An open connection to the Gods is a prize worth struggling for, but it is one that is hard won. In a world filled with moral relativism and situational ethics, it is also a gift easily lost.

Our sacred stories tell us this; they point the way for us, mapping out a road that is both exhilarating and frightening in its immensity. The Gods, by Their own struggles, show us where and how to go, just as in the story of Odin journeying to Yggdrasil and sacrificing Himself by spear and rope, for nine nights of agony, until wisdom is revealed to Him.

Our forebears lived in a world that made room for the mystical, the experiential. They lived in a world where the Gods and Goddesses were easily and openly honored. We do not. Often, we must struggle on, alone, without the presence of a spiritual community or supportive folk. So what is to keep us from despair? How do we fight the good fight spiritually? How do we bring the holy into our lives? They key may lie in an examination of the word *holiness*. From the Anglo Saxon "halig," our word *holiness* means "to make whole or healthy" (ultimately the word derives from the Proto-Indo-European root *kailo*, from which *hale*, *whole*, *health*, and *hail* are drawn). Any spiritual practitioner knows that true health is not dependent on the body and mind alone; there must be emotional and spiritual health, as well. Spiritual wholeness is maintained by devotional practices that nourish and nurture our connection with the Divine. Building spiritual health and strength is a process, very much like the strengthening of a muscle. In many ways, our awakening spirits can be likened to seeds buried deep in rich, dark earth. They must be cared for and nourished with water, sunlight, and proper care in order to grow and thrive. The same holds true for us spiritually: we must learn to sustain ourselves through disciplined practice. This discipline is, ultimately, a gift that we give ourselves. It has the power to sustain and nourish us as nothing else can, providing a lifeline through the inevitable dark night of the soul—the spiritual descent.

There are several branches in this tree of spiritual practice, each of them necessary to craft a well-balanced devotional life. I had a recent epiphany through the grace of the Goddess Frigga regarding just this. Previously, I had focused on prayer and the occasional cleansing bath, but now I realize that true spiritual wholeness is so much more. It permeates every aspect of our lives and defines (or should define) our ethics and goals. It is the rule against which everything else must be measured, if we are to truly nourish holiness and devotional consciousness within ourselves. Essentially, this means not doing that which does not nourish us spiritually, not doing that which will diminish us as spiritual beings. It means not sating every pleasure or desire, but instead looking at the larger picture, the larger tapestry of one's life, soul, and purpose. It means actively cultivating what Buddhism would term right action and right association in one's life—doing what is right, even if it means standing up and confronting a wrong. There is an old saying: God is in the details. It's from such seemingly small, insignificant things that our spiritual integrity can be forged or broken. Such discipline, such care, is largely alien to us in our dominant culture. Indeed, we are often taught exactly the opposite. It is all the more necessary then that we take pains to cultivate such mindfulness within ourselves, drawing our inspiration from wherever we can and seeking out like-minded individuals. There is no greater work that we shall ever do. This cannot be emphasized enough; the occasional ritual or reading of lore is simply not enough. Spiritual health, that which enables us to maintain a strong connection to the Gods, must be an ongoing practice. Mindfulness in everything—no matter how seemingly small—is the key to making that practice successful.

This system of devotional practice, if you will, can be separated into three primary parts: prevention, maintenance, and replenishment. These practices work together to form a balanced, vibrant whole. Neglect one, and the others inevitably suffer. It is within our abilities to become cocreators with the Gods, and as such, we are given the opportunity and tools to make our spiritual emergence easier. The beginning, especially if one is alone, without a Kindred, can often be the most terrifying. The path can seem arduous and complex, and finding a place to begin—a way to make those first faltering steps—often seems a daunting task. It need not be, however. There are, at least, some simple guidelines for navigating that labyrinth.

Firstly, it's important to remember that few of us were raised honoring the Gods and Goddesses. It's fairly safe to say that most of us were raised in one of the dominant religions of our culture: Christianity, Judaism, and possibly Islam. For many raised in the more fundamentalist denominations of these religions, coming to an awareness and love of the Gods can be a terrifying experience, often fraught with guilt. One helpful thing to remember is that our spirituality did not evolve in a vacuum; it's not a matter of suddenly excising the lessons with which we were brought up, but of evolving and adding yet another layer to the tapestry of our sacred landscape. For instance, I was raised Catholic. Though I left the church when quite young, I still draw immense spiritual nourishment from the writings of the Rhine mystics, from C.S. Lewis, and from renegade modern mystic Matthew Fox. It is from my Catholic grandmother that I first learned to value the spiritual, and from the writings of the Rhine mystics, long-dead women of a religion I no longer practice, that I learned the importance of prayer and, more importantly, how to pray. It's not an either/or scenario, and none of us go to the Gods as blank religious slates.

Therefore, for one newly emerging into Heathenry, it's important to realize that it's okay to cull the beautiful devotional aspects of one's own faith. There's nothing wrong with that. It provides a bridge to the new, and this is a good thing. While purists may rage against anything smacking of syncretization, it is often a necessary step in one's spiritual journey.[1] Moreover, there are commonalities to the spiritual experience that transcend the barriers of denomination and religion. Great comfort and understanding can be achieved by reading of shared experience—even if that experience occurs across religious lines. Find what nourishes you in your religion of birth. Find those things that help you move forward toward greater awareness of the Gods.

So it is with the third category of spiritual discipline that I will begin: replenishment. Prayer, meditation, ritual work, reading, and study—all of these things, when done with mindfulness, replenish one's spiritual vitality. Of these, I personally consider prayer to be the most important. There is a medieval proverb that goes "Lex orandi, lex credendi": the rule of prayer precedes the rule of belief. Prayer is fundamental, the first and most important building block in the road to spiritual health. It precedes everything else. It's also an act of immense courage. Prayer has the potential to change everything. It opens us to the experience of the Gods like nothing else can. It nurtures our relationship with Them as courtship nurtures the relationship between lovers. It cannot be overestimated. When we pray, we delve deeply into the heart of God as much as He or She delves deeply into us. There is an enormous reciprocity about this seemingly simple act, one that I am only now beginning to understand. It is like reaching out to grasp the hand of the Gods—an acknowledgement of one's willingness to walk with Them, to accept responsibility for acting as cocreators with the Gods in our lives. This is not necessarily a comfortable thing. It is a surrender; it brings us to the point of surrender, but what is being given up is nothing more than those blockages and doubts that keep us from truly being all that we can be. We surrender those things that keep us from standing in the source of our personal power, that keep us from being spiritually healthy or whole, and we surrender those things that keep us from truly loving and knowing the Gods.

Hand in hand with prayer goes meditation. As prayer allows us to speak to the Gods from the heart, so meditation puts us in the proper frame of mind to truly listen to Their response. There are many types of meditation: guided meditations and pathworkings; chanting and mantra work; moving meditations, such as yoga and tai chi; breathing meditations; study of sacred texts; and so on. But the first and, in my opinion, one of the most powerful meditations that one can begin with is quite simple: altar work. As human beings, we crave the sacred. We crave a palpable connection with the Divine. Nowhere is this more obvious than in the nearly universal practice of creating altars. You see them in one form or another in nearly every culture, living or dead. And in times of great tragedy or stress, they often crop up automatically. I live in New York City, and during the aftermath of 9/11, a curious phenomenon blossomed throughout the city: altars sprang up almost overnight—everywhere. Parks, churches, and the perimeter of Ground Zero were festooned with devotional shrines and offerings. And curiously, many of the offerings, left no doubt by people who had no conscious connection with their ancestors or the Gods of their ancestors, were quite traditional: coins, pictures, food, and beer (to name but a few). It was profound, wrenching, and at the same time, uplifting. It created a nexus of spiritual focus, a reservoir of power to guide the dead to their ancestral halls. A year and a half after 9/11, when city officials removed the majority of the altars, there was a definite sense of loss. Altar work is instinctual. It is healing. We create them in our homes without even realizing it, gathering those symbols that recall to us the sacredness of life. They are a source of connection, reconnection, and comfort.

Setting up a personal altar is simplicity itself. In fact, as one's spiritual practice grows, any flat space becomes fair game. Altars have this amazing tendency to grow! The entire process of creating an altar makes a statement that you are consciously inviting Deity into your life, that you are opening a door and extending an invitation. Place on an altar those things symbolic of important places in your spiritual landscape, those things that call to mind the bounty and blessings of the Gods. Pray before it regularly, light candles, and meditate, for an altar should be a living thing reflecting the spiritual evolution of its creator. There is nothing worse than seeing an altar lying stagnant and in disarray. Set aside time each day to talk with the Gods, even if it is only 10 minutes. This is the way to begin working those spiritual muscles. Ritual work is important as well, but not everyone has the means to immediately begin there. It can be too intimidating. Many people, instead of seeing ritual as a process through which the experience of the Divine is internalized, get caught up with preconceptions of static ceremony and dull repetition; or they worry about not doing things "right." Ritual is what the devotee makes of it, and learning to pray well and center one's life around the Gods is an excellent place to begin. All else will, in time, flow naturally from that beginning.

One often-neglected aspect of spiritual growth and development is volunteer work. We are all interconnected. We have a responsibility to work, in whatever capacity we can, for the well-being of our neighbors. By giving of our time and effort, we are given the powerful opportunity to become vessels of Divine energy and compassion, and we ourselves are strengthened spiritually. It also helps maintain a certain perspective when in the more painful throws of the spiritual descent. Donating blood, volunteering at a literacy center or the local soup kitchen, becoming a big brother or sister, working one day a week at a local animal shelter, volunteering a few hours a month at a nursing home or hospital are just a few of the dozens of volunteer opportunities. Giving back, contributing, and making one's community stronger is a vital and necessary part of one's spiritual development. It takes us out of ourselves, removes us, ever so slightly, from our culture-induced egotism. It can be, in many cases, the best therapy in the world.

Hand in hand with devotional work go the other two branches on our spiritual tree: prevention and maintenance. In addition to working toward a strong, spiritual connection to the Gods, part of the process of spiritual emergence involves clearing out emotional and psychic dreck. It involves a certain degree of cleansing of one's space and one's self. Most ancient religions had some laws of ritual purity for those who maintained their temples and shrines, and I'm sure we've all heard the old saying "cleanliness is next to Godliness." Well, there's some truth to that. It's more than physical cleansing, though, that is an important part of it (in feng shui, physical clutter is indicative of emotional and spiritual blockages in one's life). It is often helpful and necessary to cleanse oneself etherically as well. Be the effect of such techniques as smudging, cleansing baths, floor-washes, and the like—magical or psychological—they do aid in putting one in the proper frame of mind for spiritual work. They help us center ourselves and purge extraneous and unwanted energies and influences from our unconscious mind.

The easiest thing to do is a cleansing bath. I have often found it helpful to do special baths along with prayers for a certain number of nights. For instance, nine is Odin's sacred number. If I feel the need to clean away blockages in my relationship with Him or simply want to open more fully to His energy, I will mix up an Odin bath using herbs associated in Nordic and Anglo-Saxon lore with Him, and then take a cleansing bath for nine consecutive nights, often utilizing the same prayer each night as I bathe. It is powerfully effective. Cleansing baths are quite common in the Hoodoo tradition of the American South and crop up quite frequently in the Afro-Caribbean traditions as well, where practitioners have raised it to a high ritual art. There's no reason, however, that we can't also benefit from such a tradition. After all, there is evidence that cleansing baths were part of European folk practices as well.[2] For those uncomfortable with practices not specifically noted in the lore, smudging oneself with burning recels, such as mugwort, may be used in place of the cleansing bath. The Anglo-Saxon medical texts make reference to this practice, and these texts draw from the healing knowledge of pre-Christian Heathen culture.

When I feel the need for a major cleansing, I usually turn to the Goddess Frigga. She is extremely no-nonsense. Those who honor Frigga as their Patroness often joke about the initial requirement She demands: housecleaning. I think the reason behind this is more esoteric than one might initially think. Frigga is, in many respects, a power broker. Cleaning removes clutter and blockages, and doing so allows for a free flow of vital energy. This is necessary for health, abundance, and luck to blossom. How much more important is this then, in the realm of the spiritual?

Just as we cleanse ourselves, our homes should be given the same care. Regular floor washes, smudging, and even keeping glasses of water with a bit of ammonia in each room (changing them weekly) all encourage positive energy in the home. I'm a very hands-on person, so I gravitate toward such earthy practices. Fortunately for me (and you, too), both floor washes and sacred baths are very simple to make. Allow me to offer a basic example:

Frigga Cleansing Bath

In a large soup pot mix together the following:

> 1 cup each of: rosemary, basil, cinnamon (sticks are fine), lavender, chamomile, rue, sage, and fresh-squeezed lime juice.[3]
>
> Add 2–3 gallons of spring water and bring to a boil. Remove from heat. Let sit until cool, then cover and refrigerate.

For seven consecutive days, take a soothing bath, adding a cup of sea salt to the water. AFTER you bathe, pour 2 cups of the herbal mixture (strained into a container) over your body. This is the traditional way to take a cleansing bath. First you take a regular bath, THEN you pour the cleansing mixture over your head and body. As you do so, ask Frigga to cleanse you of any blockages or negativity that may be holding you back spiritually. To make a floor wash, simply add one cup of ammonia to the blend and add it to your bucket of mop water. This need only be done once, not seven consecutive days.

Practices such as this, though simple, involve all our senses. I am an extremely kinetic person, so I prefer those techniques that incorporate not only sight (a beautiful altar) or sound (singing a prayer), but also smell, feeling, and at times, movement. I strongly believe that devotional work should speak not only to the mind but that it should be a full-body experience. So incorporate regular cleansing into your spiritual routine, even if only a weekly housecleaning and smudging with sage or asperging with an infusion of basil or marjoram around the perimeter of each room (both are said to bring happiness and peace). This is good preventive medicine. It's like taking a daily vitamin. It keeps sluggish and unhealthy energies away. The same can be said of using a Tibetan bowl to smudge a room or playing sacred music before meditation or ritual to "set the mood." I often think that the process of spiritual emergence is an ongoing fight against entropy. These are tools at our disposal that will give us the metaphorical upper hand against that insidious foe.

The third and final category of spiritual self-maintenance is the realm of warding and maintaining one's spiritual boundaries. In doing so, we make of ourselves a sacred enclosure welcoming to the Gods and beneficial to our own selves. This encompasses not only right association and right action, as noted previously, but also warding and shielding oneself from spiritual harm. There are numerous books on the market with daunting titles, such as *Psychic Self-Defense* by Dion Fortune and *Practical Guide to Psychic Self-Defense and Well-Being* by Melita Denning. What these works really teach are the techniques whereby we retain our spiritual and psychic integrity. These practices are a necessity not only for spiritual health but for mental and emotional health, as well. Grounding, centering, and basic wardings of both self and home are fundamental. In many ways, all of these practices come down to choosing to center one's life around the Gods and filtering all other experiences and choices through that lens of spiritual devotion.

In reality, that's the key to spiritual emergence: consciously centering one's life around the Gods. Everything else is decoration. The devotee who keeps that goal foremost in his or her mind will find the spiritual process far, far easier in the long run. We are spiritual beings. It's a difficult thing to remember in a world that emphasizes anything but. We are challenged to holiness. And we are challenged not only to make ourselves holy and to recognize our spiritual callings, but to carry that awareness into our daily lives, to everyone we touch. It is a difficult task. Moreover, it is one that we must do over and over again, in a never-ending process. We are growing toward the Gods.

Our tools in this journey are simple ones: prayer, meditation, service, compassion, strength, discipline, and courage. But what wonders they reveal if adhered to with assiduous focus! There is a wonderful quote by medieval Christian mystic Meister Eckhart that beautifully sums up the spiritual journey: "Be ready. Be aware. God is a thousand, thousand times more ready to give than we are to receive." I would add that the Gods, in my experience are amazing opportunists. If we but give Them the smallest opening, They will surge forth, filling our hearts and minds with Their presence and love. Perseverance, reverence, and devotion are the keys on this royal road of wisdom. Holiness is nothing more than the ongoing discipline of spiritual mindfulness, and to that we can all aspire.

Chapter 10

Holy Tides

Like any other religion, Heathenry has its holy days. Generally, these holidays, called *holy tides*, follow the cycle of the seasons and natural year. This is because people's lives in preindustrial civilizations depended on the rhythms of the earth—ploughing, planting, and harvesting—for survival. The most important holidays fall on either the solstices or the equinoxes. In fact, at least to Anglo-Saxon Heathens, the entire year was broken up into 10 months, each defined by either agricultural or holy work done during that time. Celebrations were usually held on the eve of the holiday in question.

Yule

According to Branston,[1] "the last month of the old year and the first of the new were together called Giuli (Yule)." The most sacred and important of all Heathen holy celebrations falls within this span of time and is called *Modraniht*, or Mothers' Night—a celebration honoring the tribal Goddesses and one's powerful Dísir. As in ancient times, this rite is usually held on the Winter Solstice, which usually falls between December 22 and 25. Many modern Christmas customs, such as the giving of gifts and the raising of a tree, were actually remnants from earlier Heathen practices.

Yule is a celebration replete with feasting and gift-giving, and it is one of the holidays during which traditional sacrifices, such as the sonargöltr,[2] to the Gods are made. It is a time when Woden is said to ride freely through the skies at the head of the Wild Hunt, ever ready to gather the souls of the unwary. It is also a time when the veil between the realms of the living and the realms of the dead is thin and strong communication may be made with one's ancestors. In addition to blóting to the Gods (usually Woden, Thunor, Frigga, Frey), at least one day of celebration should be devoted to the ancestors.

Yule is a liminal time of great power. The 12 days of Yule celebration (December 25 through January 6), spanning the end of one season and the beginning of another, are more powerful than any other time of year. It is a time for resolution of old debts and a laying of new wyrd, a time when fate may consciously be turned. The most elaborate feasts and high Symbel are held throughout Yule time, and it is a time of frith and mighty oath-taking. Oaths taken during this time are among the most binding and holiest of all utterances. Work—particularly work associated with Frigga, such as spinning and weaving—would cease during this holy time and the last sheaves of hay left in the fields were given in offering to Woden's horse, Sleipnir, to honor (and likely pacify) the Wild Hunt. Gifts were traditionally exchanged throughout the holiday season. The figure of Santa Clause evolved from Odin as Julfaðr and Wish-Giver.

Charming of the Plough

The next month—roughly our February—was called Solmonath: Sun Month. This was a time when the land was blessed and offerings made (usually bread or pastry) to ready it for planting in the months to come. Ploughs and field implements would also be blessed, a ritual that survived into the Christian era. Today, because the majority of Heathens no longer depend on the land for their livelihood, this holiday has been expanded to include any implement of work or creativity, including laptops, cars, and business ledgers. It's a time to honor our ability not only to support ourselves by right means, but also the means by which we leave our mark in the world. It's a time to celebrate the renewal of the creative spark—in the land and in our minds and hearts.

Ostara/Eostre

Solmonath is followed by Hreðe and Eostre (March and April, respectively), both named after Goddesses. The holy tide that falls during this time is also called *Eostre* or *Ostara*. Modern Heathens usually celebrate Ostara on or around the Spring Equinox, which usually falls at the end of March. It may also be celebrated the first full moon AFTER the equinox. Many contemporary Easter customs and symbols, such as decorating eggs and the folk-image of the "Easter Bunny" (both symbols of fertility), come from the Heathen holiday. Unsurprisingly, just as the Charming of the Plough honors those tools that work the land, so Ostara honors the fecundity of the land itself, the quickening of the seed within the dark earth, and the coming of Spring.

Eostre/Ostara is a time of renewal and rebirth. It's an excellent time to embark upon new projects. It's also a good time for cleaning and cleansing—perhaps the real reason the idea of "spring cleaning" came into being! Ostara is a time to bid goodbye to winter.

Walpurgisnacht

The month of May, according to the old Anglo-Saxon calendar, was called *Thrimilci*, because this month was traditionally a time of plenty, when the cows could be milked three times a day and, in contrast to the leaner time of winter, food and milk were plentiful.

Walpurgisnacht is quite an unusual holiday, generally celebrated on April 30. Traditionally, it is seen as a time when witches ride and dangerous beings gather to feast. The Goddess Holda is strongly associated with this feast, as is Freya. Charms and prayers for the protection of livestock and the fields would be offered, and bonfires were often kindled atop mountains to honor these mighty beings. Walpurgis was also a time of courtship and romance, and it is in this way that it survives amongst modern Heathens—unsurprising, if we remember that Freya is a Goddess of both witchcraft and attraction. This holiday is a fitting time to honor romantic partners and friends—all the loves in one's life. It's a time to celebrate the flowering of relationships and to pray for fertility, not necessarily of body but of those relationships in general. Offerings may be left for Vaettir and Etins, to ward off ill luck, but gifts may also be given to loved ones and friends. This is a joyous holiday, and its symbols are those of fertility and sexuality: wreaths of flowers, bonfires, and of course, the maypole—a phallic symbol if ever there was one. Of course, the maypole may also be a stand-in for the World Tree—the axis of power that supports all life. Either way, Walpurgis is a celebration of life, plenty, and passion.

Litha

This leads us into our next holy tide: Midsummer. The months of June and July were called *Litha*, which may mean "moon,"[3] and Midsummer was celebrated on the Summer Solstice, at the end of June. It is second only to Yule in being the most important holiday, regardless of denomination, to Heathens both ancient and modern. First and foremost, it is a celebration of summer and of the luck and wealth of the folk. Thanks are given for health and prosperity, and prayers offered for continued might in the coming year. Traditional rites, just as at Yule, would often include the sacrifice of a pig to the God Freyr, in gratitude for the community's abundance and good fortune.

Midsummer is a fire festival, and bonfires were an integral part of ancient celebration. Offerings, including the remnants of the sacrificial pig, were tossed into the fire as gifts to the Gods. This holiday is a time when Heathens celebrate the rebirth of their faith, their connection as folk, and their connection to the Gods of their ancestors.

Hlæfmæst

At the end of July, usually on the full moon or sometimes the very last day of July, modern Heathens celebrate the harvest. This is really a modern practice drawn from a number of harvest festivals celebrated in pre-Christian England and Germany. There was no one, large, universal harvest celebration at this time, but smaller, regional celebrations were common. Sometimes this holiday is referred to as *Freyfaxi*, and sometimes *Lammas*, which literally translates as "loaf-mass." According to Swain Wodening,[4] this month may have been sacred to Thor, and another name for it was *Thunormonath*. Rites celebrated at this time generally honor the preceding bounty of the harvest. Offerings are given to the Gods and Vaettir, partly in thanks and partly in the hopes of a healthy and safe winter. Traditions include making bread, fashioned in the shape of a man, for both feasting and offering. According to the agricultural calendar, this was the time when the fields would be threshed and grain harvested. It was also the time when folk would begin putting away stores for the winter months. Modern Heathens often connect this particular feast to the story of Loki cropping Sif's hair, connecting the shearing of Her hair to the act of harvesting grain.

August was referred to as *Weodmonath*: month of weeds. No holy tides falls during this time.

Haligmonath

The month of September was called *Haligmonath* or "holy month." It is another harvest holiday, which is generally celebrated at the Autumnal Equinox in late September. It is very akin to a Heathen Thanksgiving, continuing the theme of giving thanks for the bounty of the preceding harvest. It is the last great feast before the winter months and Yule. This was also the month of offerings of all types. Folk would make offerings in thanksgiving for luck, health, and wealth experienced during the previous year, but also to ensure a fruitful harvest in the year to come. These offerings were a way of giving something back to the Gods, of recognizing and honoring all that we receive from Their hands. The process of celebrating the holy tides and making offerings makes each and every person a partner in the unfolding cycle of their wyrd. It is at this holiday that Heathens celebrate their part in that cycle of life.

Winter Nights/Winterfyllith

The month of October was called *Winterfyllith*. It was a time when Heathens made offerings to their dead and remembered their ancestors in feasting, stories, and sacred rites. Modern Heathens generally celebrate Winter Nights as a day of the dead. The Dísir and Álfar are given offerings, usually a complete feast. Their stories are told, they are hailed in fainings, and it is generally seen, like the Celtic celebration of Samhain, as a time when the veil between the world of the living and the world of the dead is thin. Ancestral veneration is a foundational tenet of Heathenry, and the ancestors provide strength, luck, and blessings to the folk. This holiday is a time to repay those gifts with offerings, rituals, and mindful attention to the dead. For those seeking specific wisdom from their ancestors, there is no better time to facilitate communication.

Winter Nights is also the time heralding the arrival of winter. Many Heathens choose to hail Deities associated with the winter months at this time, such as Skaði and Ullr. This holiday begins a cycle of introspection and reflection, culminating with the 12 nights of Yule. It is a time to make amends for any ill actions committed, wrap up unfinished projects, and take stock of one's choices and actions the preceding year.

The month of November is called *Blótmonath*: "blood month." Though no holidays fall during this month, it was a time when the surplus livestock were butchered in preparation for the winter. Today it is not uncommon to hold fainings and blótar to Woden, Freyr, and Thor during this time. Additionally, Veteran's Day falls in November, and it is nearly a universal day of remembrance for modern Heathens. Fainings are held to honor the *Einherjar*, warriors who have fallen in battle and, thus, earned their place in Valhalla in Odin's army. Ancestors who have served in the military, living relatives who serve, as well as loved ones left behind, are all named and honored. Memorial Day is another day of remembrance observed as a holy day in the Heathen community. Military service is considered a great honor amongst modern Heathens, and veterans are highly respected for their courage and sacrifice.

In addition to the major holy tides, many Heathens celebrate feast days of heroes and heroines celebrated in Heathen history and lore. Figures such as Penda, the last great Heathen King of Mercia, and Queen Sigrid the proud, who refused a marriage proposal from Olaf Tryggvason (a figure loathed by modern Heathens for his attempts to convert the folk to Christianity by any means necessary), are often honored for their deeds, as well as for the inspiration they give to modern Heathens. The format of the rites celebrated on the holy tides does not differ considerably from the basic faining, Symbel, or blót. It is the intent and the nature of the prayers made and offerings given that determines the difference.

Chapter Notes

Introduction

[1] Though many Fellowship of Isis Iseums and Lyceums are Wiccan, the organization as a whole is not a Wiccan organization.

[2] Though some Heathens might disagree, I tend to use *Odin*, *Oðinn*, and *Woden* interchangeably.

[3] It's commonly believed that to wear the valknot is to dedicate oneself irrevocably as a living sacrifice to Odin, to be claimed at His will and at the time of His choosing.

[4] There is an ongoing debate in Heathen circles about whether Heathen clergy should be trained in counseling. Some prefer to restrict the role of the Heathen priest to ceremonial, sacrificial, and ritual performance. Others, like myself, favor a more service-oriented approach in which counseling forms a very definite basis.

[5] Former Catholic priest Matthew Fox was defrocked in 1989 for "consorting with Witches," because of his long-standing professional association with modern Witch Starhawk. The controversy surrounding his book *Coming of the Cosmic Christ* and his stance in favor of creation spirituality had much to do with his dismissal. He was later accepted into the Episcopalian priesthood.

[6] While syncretization is one thing, it is important to guard against cultural misappropriation or "strip-mining." Worship of our Gods

and Goddesses evolved in specific cultural contexts. Their sacred stories and symbols reflect this. Out of respect, learn about the culture in which worship of our Gods initially evolved. Guard against transposing 20th-century ethics onto ancient cultural markers. Strive to meet the God or Goddess on His or Her own ground. It is respectful to the Deity and the tradition. Don't mix and match.

Chapter 1

[1] Tacitus p. 109.

[2] K.C. Hulsman, Section 1.1 "The Viking Age."

[3] Thomas Duboise, *Nordic Religions in the Viking Age* (University of Pennsylvania Press, 1999).

[4] Jones, Prudence and Nigel Pennick, p. 156.

[5] Olaf Tryggvason ruled Norway from 995–999 C.E. His name is reviled amongst modern Heathens for the violence and cruelty with which he forced conversion on his people.

[6] Swain Wodening, *Hammer of the Gods*, p. 10.

[7] Some historical accounts give 999 C.E. as the date in question, but 1000 C.E. is the most commonly accepted date.

[8] Utiseta—a common Nordic system of divination, meditation, and wisdom-seeking wherein the seeker would isolate him- or herself literally underneath a cloak or animal skin for a given period of time.

[9] John Lindow, a respected scholar in the field of Norse Mythology, commented in his book *Norse Mythology* (Oxford Press, 2001) that "there was a revival of 'belief in the aesir' some years ago in Iceland, which seemed to have to do at least in part with tax breaks for organized religion, although partying is also important. That revival had its counterpart in Norway, where a group of students announced themselves to be believers in the aesir. In celebration, they drank some beer and sacrificed a sausage," p. 38. This is not an uncommon attitude among modern scholars.

[10] 2001 Asatru Folk Assembly online Article, "Hitlerism v. Odinism," found online at *www.runestone.org/lep4.html*.

[11] Hulsman, section 1.3.

[12] *Asatru* means "faith in the Gods" and is one of the largest branches of Heathenry. Its practitioners draw largely from Icelandic sources for religious inspiration.

[13] Tribal law or custom.

[14] A rooftree issue is any issue that belongs in the realm of one's home, does not affect the community, and is, to be frank, none of the community's business.

Chapter 2

[1] The best Eddic sources for Heathen cosmology are the "Voluspa," "Grimnismal," and "Vafthrudnismal."

[2] H.R. Ellis Davidson, *Gods and Myths of Northern Europe*, p. 199.

[3] Bauschatz p. 5.

[4] Snorri Sturluson, *Poetic Edda*, "Voluspa," Taylor and Auden translation, pp. 147–148.

[5] Lindow p. 254, quoting from "Voluspa."

Chapter 3

[1] I have provided the Anglo-Saxon names, where known or reconstructed, in parenthesis following the better known Norse appellations.

[2] Krasskova p. 24.

[3] A comprehensive list of His heiti, or bynames may be found online at *www.angelfire.com/on/Wodensharrow/odennamn.html*.

[4] Personal correspondence with Wulfgaest, Heah Aeweweard of the Ealdriht.

[5] From the Old Norse verb *gala*, "to croak or to crow."

[6] H.R. Ellis Davidson, *Gods and Myths of Northern Europe*, p. 70.

[7] Modern Heathen lore is comprised of the Elder Edda; Younger Edda; Icelandic Sagas; Anglo-Saxon Healing Texts; law codes and histories; and current anthropological, archeological, and historical analysis.

[8] Snorri Sturluson, *The Poetic Edda*, translated by C. Larrington p. 34.

[9] Translated by D.L. Ashliman, Ph.D.: *www.pitt.edu/~dash/merseburg.html*.

[10] *The Lacnunga Manuscript* quoted from *Leechcraft* by Stephen Pollington (Anglo-Saxon Books, 2000), p. 217.

[11] Snorri Sturluson, *The Poetic Edda*, translated by C. Larrington, p. 35.

[12] Such as when He summons the seeress forth in the Voluspa and commands her to scry the future for Him.

[13] *Gods of the North* by Brian Branston p. 112.

[14] Sun Tzu p. 18.

[15] Now it is hardly agreed upon by scholars whether or not the Norse even had Shamanic practitioners, but it is an intriguing theory none the less.

[16] Simek points out that Grimm was sceptical of this, as there is wild moss (*Polytrichum aureum*) whose name in Old Norse translates as "Sif's hair."

[17] Private e-mail correspondence.

[18] Oðins Korpgalder, available online at *www.northvegr.org*.

[19] *Poetic Edda*, "Griminismal."

[20] K.C. Hulsman.

[21] Jan de Vries, volume II.

[22] Ordeal by combat.

[23] "Teiwas—His Law and Order in Middle Earth" by Dan O'Halloran.

[24] Snorri Sturluson, *Prose Edda*, translated by Jean Young, p. 59.

[25] Snorri Sturluson, *Poetic Edda*, translated by Lee Hollander, p. 150.

[26] Pronounced *Air*, like the element.

[27] Simek pp. 71–72.

[28] Simek pp. 71–72.

[29] Anglo Saxon for "healer." See *Leechcraft* by Stephen Pollington.

[30] Ibid.

[31] Common in Anglo-Saxon and Germanic healing theory, sudden pain in the bones and joints, arthritis, and rheumatism were often said to be caused by poisoned darts shot into the patient by unseen beings common to the natural world. It was also used to describe certain types of magical attack.

[32] Along with Bald's LeecIhbok, the LacnIunga forms the largest surviving body of Anglo-Saxon healing lore.

[33] There is some evidence that early Germanic tribes had a system of healing very similar to Chinese acupuncture.

[34] In Nordic lore, the dead—particularly strong female ancestors—are known to grant healing wisdom and advice.

[35] According to Snorri Sturluson's *Poetic Edda*, Her handmaidens are Hlíf (Protection), Blíð (Blithe), and Fríð (Right Order, Peace).

[36] Simek p. 309.

[37] Snorri Sturluson, *Poetic Edda*, translated by Hollander, "Voluspa."

[38] Simek p. 191.

[39] Simek p. 227.

[40] Simek pp. 135–136.

[41] The scholar Dumezil speculates that Heimdall is a God of long life, symbolized by His birth of nine mothers, however, He just as likely may be connected to the concept of reincarnation and rebirth.

[42] I have heard it speculated that Loki and Heimdall are inextricably connected, because They each contain complementary power: Loki possesses the destructive power of fire, the catalytic power of unexpected change. Heimdall possesses the nourishing power of fire, its warmth and life-giving properties, and balanced, guided change.

[43] Within Neoweanglia Maethel, Heimdall is the Patron of the School of Theodish Studies, the Contemplatives Guild.

[44] *Vé*, *hörgr*, or *hof*—from Swain Wodening, *Hammer of the Gods*, p. 81.

[45] H.R. Ellis Davidson, *Gods and Myths of Northern Europe* p. 168.

[46] Man-price, the legal debt paid to the kin of one slain in lieu of further blood being spilled.

[47] "Ynglinga Saga," Chapter 8.

[48] Tacitus, Chapter 40.

[49] Sheffield p. 35.

[50] Simek p. 105.

[51] Ordered powers, another name for the panoply of Gods within the Northern Tradition.

[52] Simek p. 195.

[53] Multiple private correspondence.

[54] Private correspondence.

[55] Swain Wodening, *Hammer of the Gods*, p. 79.

[56] Simek p. 260.

[57] Because alcohol plays such an important role in Heathen religious rites, many Heathens home brew beer and especially mead.

[58] Swain Wodening, *Hammer of the Gods*, p. 88.

[59] *Marklander Journal*, #75, volume X, #3.

[60] Called a *vé* in Old Norse, or *weofod* in Anglo-Saxon.

[61] Simek p. 276.

[62] Snorri Sturluson, *Prose Edda*, Young p. 61.

[63] Simek p. 201.

[64] Aecerbot, a blessing of the fields, is one of the few surviving Anglo-Saxon charms/prayers wherein an actual Heathen Deity is openly invoked. The page where I first located it is no longer part of the *www.ealdriht.org* Web site, although it is referenced in Swain Wodening's *Hammer of the Gods*, p. 87.

[65] Not to be confused with the male God Fjorgynn, father of Frigga.

[66] Simek p. 229.

[67] Taken from the Latin *necare*, "to kill," and *helan*, "to hide."

Chapter 4

[1] Bauschatz p. 5.

[2] Eliade p. 380, 383.

[3] Snorri Sturluson, *The Poetic Edda*, translated by Larrington, pp. 3–27.

[4] Bauschatz p. 6.

[5] Snorri Sturluson, *Poetic Edda*, translated by Larrington, "Grimnismal" pp. 87–106.

[6] Dubois pp. 122–138.

[7] Bauschatz p. 9.

[8] The Norn of the future, of that which becomes.

[9] Bauschatz p. 13.

[10] This is one of the fundamental cosmological concepts of any Shamanic tradition. Dubois pp. 122–138.

[11] Personified by Verdandi/Verdande.

[12] Bauschatz p. 16.

[13] The old Norse concept of personal prosperity, luck, and might passed from one generation to the next. Like orlog, it could be affected by a person's choices and actions.

[14] In Norse theology, one's Hamingja, or luck, is said to form part of the soul matrix.

[15] Bauschatz p. 19.

[16] *The Prose Edda.*
[17] Bauschatz p. 19.
[18] Bauschatz p. 21.
[19] Ibid.
[20] Bauschatz p. 23.

Chapter 5

[1] The Norse word is given first, followed by the Anglo-Saxon.
[2] Swain Wodening, *Hammer of the Gods,* p. 52.
[3] *Runelore,* p. 168.
[4] Swain Wodening, *Hammer of the Gods,* p. 55.
[5] Burial mound.
[6] One of the Afro-Caribbean religions.
[7] I would point out that honoring one's ancestors is not an excuse for racism. Everyone has ancestors, and they and their cultures should be celebrated.
[8] I have, on one occasion, had trouble with a meddlesome dead aunt who was fretful about my religion. I told her point blank that if she wants to be honored in my house, she will respect my religious choice, and I pointed her toward some more enlightened relatives who could explain things to her. Just because a person is dead does not mean he or she is all-knowing. If an ancestor is causing problems, he or she can be uninvited.
[9] Some folk will use an Anglicized version of this term, *wight* or *wights*. It has nothing to do with race, however, and is a poor adaptation of the original Norse terminology.

Chapter 6

[1] The "Havamal" is part of the *Poetic Edda*. In it, Oðinn offers wise counsel on how to live a good and honorable life.
[2] Elder Eric Wodening wrote a very important book titled *We are Our Deeds*, which explores ethics and thew within modern Heathenry. It is an invaluable resource.
[3] Swain Wodening, *Hammer of the Gods,* pp. 41–43.

[4] In fact, according to pre-Christian Germanic ethics, taking up the bloodfeud to avenge the murder of a relative might be considered a means of restoring the frith.

Chapter 7

[1] Simek pp. 271–272.

[2] The Braga-full, over which vows and sacred oaths were made. This has survived in the modern Heathen practice of Symbel, in which a horn filled with alcohol is passed around three times: once to honor the Gods, once to honor ancestors, and once to make sacred vows or boasts. A vow taken over the horn is especially sacred within Heathen tradition.

[3] "Hakon the Good's Saga" from *Heimskringla* by Snorri Sturluson. The excerpt here is taken from a version published by the Norroena Society, London, 1907. This version may be found online at *www.northvegr.org/lore/heim/index.html*.

[4] Right order, harmony, peace.

[5] From the "Sigdrifumal," *Poetic Edda*, my paraphrase.

[6] One's personal, ancestral luck.

[7] Available in Edred Thorsson's *Futhark*.

[8] Available in Swain Wodening's *Hammer of the Gods*.

[9] Krasskova p. 18.

Chapter 8

[1] Murphy p. 149 and 67, respectively.

[2] The most common example being the Goddess (and saint) Brigid.

[3] *The Meadhall*, Stephen Pollington, p. 47.

[4] Chickering, lines 491–495 and 615–630.

[5] Numerous scholarly works have been written examining the role of women in Symbel and within the warband, most notably *Wealhtheow and the Valkyrie Tradition* by Helen D'Amico and *Lady With a Mead Cup* by Michael Enright.

[6] Tacitus p. 108.

[7] Hulsman p. 70.

[8] Theodish Heathenry is an orthodox denomination that adheres to tribal structure and thew.

[9] Private e-mail correspondence.

[10] Hulsman p. 73.

[11] Private e-mail correspondence.

[12] *The Whisperings of Woden* by Galina Krasskova (Global Book Publishers, 2004). Available through *www.amazon.com.*

[13] *The Meadhall,* Pollington p. 54.

[14] Ibid.

[15] Swain Wodening, *Hammer of the Gods,* p. 134.

[16] Snorri Sturlason, *Poetic Edda*, translated by C. Larrington, p. 24.

[17] *The Meadhall,* Pollington p. 53.

Chapter 9

[1] While syncretization is one thing, it is important to guard against cultural misappropriation or "strip-mining." Worship of our Gods and Goddesses evolved in specific cultural contexts. Their sacred stories and symbols reflect this. Many, such as Kali, Amaterasu, Kuan Yin, and Oshun, are still worshipped today in essentially an unbroken line of practice. Out of respect, when honoring a Deity, learn about the culture in which His or Her worship initially evolved. Guard against transposing 20th-century ethics onto ancient cultural markers. Strive to meet the God or Goddess on His or Her own ground. It is respectful to the Deity and the tradition. Don't mix and match.

[2] Mickaharic, *Spiritual Cleansing*, pp. 16–17.

[3] Thanks to Jason Barnes, Frey's-man and goði, for this bath recipe.

Chapter 10

[1] *Lost Gods of England* by Brian Branston, p. 51.

[2] Sacrificial Yule pig.

[3] *Lost Gods of England* by Brian Branston, p. 52

[4] Swain Wodening, *Hammer of the Gods,* p. 116.

Glossary

Æsir: [*Eye´ seer*] The primary tribe of Gods, often associated with wisdom, order, justice, and knowledge. Odin, Thor, and Frigga were numbered amongst the Æsir. The word *Ás* itself means "God."

Álfar: [*Owl´ far*] Male ancestors. This word may also be used to indicate elves or inhabitants of Alfheim.

Beot: [*Bay oat*] An oath or vow taken over the horn in Symbel.

Blót: [*Bloat*] A sacred ritual involving the sacrifice of a sacred animal to the Gods. Some Heathens use this word to indicate any ritual done to honor the Gods wherein a horn is passed among participants.

Dísir: [*Dee´ seer*] Powerful female ancestors. The singular is *Dís*.

Ealu bora: [*ay´ ah loo boor´ ah*] The Anglo-Saxon word for the woman who carries the horn in Symbel.

Etin: Another word for a Jotun.

Faining: A basic ritual honoring the Gods that does *not* include the sacrifice of an animal.

Frith: Right order, security, and peace enjoyed while among one's own folk, where all are adhering to the same social and ethical codes.

Gefrain: [*Yeh´ frane*] Reputation.

Gielp: [*yee elp*] A boast made over the horn in Symbel.

Ginungagap: The primal void from which all life evolved.

Hamingja: [*Ha´ ming yah*] One's personal luck.

Heiti: [*Hay´ tee*] Praise names or bynames.

Innangarð: [*In an garth*] The sacred enclosure of one's community and society bounded by thew.

Jotuns: [*Joh´ tuns*] Beings of chaos often at war with the Gods.

Maegen: [*May´ gen*] One's personal might, vitality, and lifeforce.

Maethel: [*May´ thel* or *math´ el*] A regional group of households, individuals, and Kindreds united by hold oath to a Lord.

Nornir: The three weavers of fate and destiny who lay the strands of wyrd for each individual. Their names are Urd/Urð/Urða, Verðande, and Skuld/Skulda.

Orlog: One's individual strand of wyrd.

Rooftree: Under one's own roof. When something is referred to as a "rooftree issue" it means that it is not subject to the dictates of tribal thew, but a matter of personal choice, within an individual household, and as such, cannot be gainsayed by a tribal elder without a violation of one's freedom of conscience.

Scop: [*Shope*] Bard.

Shild/Scyld: [*Shild*] Debt or obligation of honor.

Symbel: [Anglo Saxon: *Sim´ bell*, Norse: *Some´ bell*] The most sacred of Heathen rites.

Symbelgerefa: [*Sim´ bel yer ef ah*] Host or Hostess of Symbel.

Thew: Custom, observance, tribal/community law.

Thyle: [*Thill*] Lawspeaker; one who has an exceptional understanding of lore, thew, and ritual practice. The Thyle has the responsibility to ensure that improper oaths and boasts are not accepted in Symbel, thereby protecting the tribal luck.

Utgarð: [*Oot´ garth*] Those places that lie outside of the community and outside of thew.

Vaettir: [*Vy´ teer*, often mispronounced "*veht´ teer*"] Land spirits analogous to the Japanese kami. They are often associated with natural places or phenomena. Certain types of Vaettir inhabit houses and homes as well. The singular is "Vaet" [pronounced *Vight*]. Some English-speaking Heathens use the word "wight" insead. This does not in any way indicate a racial bias, but is a corruption of the original Norse term.

Valkyrie: The Norse word for the woman who bears the horn during Symbel; also, fierce female warrior beings who ride in Oðinn's battle retinue, choosing those who will die and join Oðinn in Valhalla.

Vanir: [*Vahn´ neer*] One of the tribes of Gods often associated with fertility, abundance, wealth, and sexual pleasure. Frey, Freya, and Njord are numbered amongst the Vanir.

Weonde: [*Weh´ on deh*] A song of hallowing chanted before Anglo-Saxon style Heathen rites. It blesses and hallows the space. The song is chanted as fire is carried clockwise about the space.

Wyrd: [*Weird*] Fate, causality, and consequence; that which governs every person's life.

Yggdrasil: [*Eeg´ drah seel*] The World Tree; Odin hung for nine days and nights on this Tree to win the runes. The word means "Steed of Yggr." Yggr is a byname of Odin, and the Tree is referred to as His steed because it was the means by which He gained the ability to travel between worlds.

Bibliography

Adalsteinsson, Jón. *Under the Cloak: A Pagan Ritual Turning Point in the Conversion of Iceland*. Edited by Jakob S. Jónsson. Translated by Terry Gunnell. Reykjavik: University of Iceland Press, 1999.

Asatru Folk Assembly. "Asatru/Odinism: A Briefing for Law Enforcement Officials." http://www.runestone.org/lep1.html (accessed September 21, 2003).

Ashliman, D.L. "Merseburg Incantations." http://www.pitt.edu/~dash/merseburg.html (accessed September 24, 2004).

Bauschatz, Paul. *The Well and the Tree*. Boston: University of Massachusetts Press, 1982.

Blain, Jenny. *Wights and Ancestors*. Wiltshire, England: Wyrd's Well Press, 2000.

Branston, Brian. *Gods of the North*. New York: Thames and Hudson, Inc., 1980.

———. *The Lost Gods of England:* London: Thames and Hudson, Inc., 1974.

Chickering, Howell D., trans. *Beowulf*. New York: Anchor Books, 1989.

Cook, Robert, trans. *Njál's Saga*. London: Penguin Books, 2001.

Crossley-Holland, Kevin. *The Norse Myths*. New York: Pantheon Books, 1980.

Davidson, Hilda R. Ellis. *Gods and Myths of Northern Europe*. Harmondsworth: Penguin Books, 1964.

———. "Hostile Magic in the Icelandic Sagas." In *The Witch Figure: Folklore Essays by a Group of Scholars in England Honouring the 75th Birthday of Katharine M. Briggs*, edited by Venetia Newall. Boston: Shambala, 1988.

———. *Pagan Scandinavia*. London: Thames & Hudson, 1967.

de Vries, Jan. *Altgermanische Religionsgeschichte*, late ed. Vol. 2. Berlin: Walter de Gruyter & Co., 1970.

Dubois, Thomas. *Nordic Religions in the Viking Age*. Philadelphia: University of Pennsylvania Press, 1999.

Eliade, Mircea. *Shamanism: Archaic Techniques of Ecstasy*. Translated by William Trask. Princeton, N.J.: Princeton University Press, 1964.

Enright, Michael. *The Lady with a Mead Cup: Ritual, Prophecy, and Lordship in the European Warband from La Tene to the Viking Age*. Dublin: Four Courts Press, 1996.

Federal Bureau of Investigation. "Project Megiddo." Strategic assessment of the potential for domestic terrorism in the United States, posted by Center for Studies on New Religions, http://www.cesnur.org/testi/FBI_004.htm (accessed April 2, 2003).

Glosecki, Stephen. *Shamanism and Old English Poetry*. New York: Garland Publishing, 1989.

Gundarsson, Kveldulf. *Teutonic Religion*. St. Paul, Minn.: Llewellyn Publications, 1993.

Hastrup, Kirsten. *Culture and History in Medieval Iceland: An Anthropological Analysis of Structure and Change*. Oxford, England: Oxford University Press, 1985.

———. *A Place Apart: An Anthropological Study of the Icelandic World*. Oxford, England: Clarendon Press, 1998.

Herbert, Kathleen. *Peace-Weavers and Shield-Maidens*: Wiltshire, England: Anglo-Saxon Books, 1997.

Hulsman, K.C. *Heathen Magicoreligious Practices: From the Ancient Past Through the Reconstructed Present*. Arlington, Tex.: University of Texas Press, 2004.

Jesch, Judith. *Women in the Viking Age*. Woodbridge, Suffolk: Boydell Press, 1991.

Johnston, George, trans. *The Saga of Gisli the Outlaw*. Edited by Peter Foote. Toronto: University of Toronto Press, 1963.

Jones, Prudence, and Nigel Pennick. *A History of Pagan Europe*. New York: Routledge, 2003.

Krasskova, Galina. *The Whisperings of Woden*. New York: Global Book publishers, 2004.

Kvideland, Reimund and Henning Sehmsdorf, eds. *Nordic Folklore*. Bloomington, Ind.: Indiana University Press, 1990.

Lewis, I.M. *Ecstatic Religion: A Study of Shamanism and Spirit Possession*. New York: Penguin, 1971.

Lindow, John. *Norse Mythology*. Oxford, England: Oxford University Press, 2001.

Lord, Garman. "The Ásatrú Movement." *Marklander* 61 (2002): 8–10.

———. *A Short History of Anglo-Saxon Theodism*. Watertown, N.Y.: Theod, 1994.

———. "Tomorrow's Reawakening." *Marklander* 58 (2002): 10–11.

McQueen, Gert. "A Short History of Anglo-Saxon Theodism." Watertown, N.Y.: Theod Press, 1994. http://www.geocities.com/theodish_belief/articles3.html (accessed October 4, 2004).

Mickaharic, Draja. *Spiritual Cleansing*. York Beach, Maine: Weiser Books, 1982.

Miller, William. *Bloodtaking and Peacemaking: Feud, Law, and Society in Saga Iceland*. Chicago: University of Chicago Press, 1990.

Murphy, Ronald. *The Heliand.* New York: Oxford University Press, 1992.

O'Halloran, Dan. "Teiwas—His Law and Order in Middle Earth." *Idunna: A Journal of the Northern Tradition* 54 (winter 2002–2003): 11.

Owen, Gale. *Rites and Religions of the Anglo-Saxons*. New York: Barnes and Noble Books, 1981.

Pálsson, Hermann, trans. *Eyrbyggja Saga*. London: Penguin Books, 1989.

Pollington, Stephen. *Leechcraft: Early English Charms, Plantlore and Healing.* Trowbridge: Anglo-Saxon Books, 2000.

———. *The Meadhall.* Norfolk, England: Anglo-Saxon Books, 2003.

Scudder, Bernard, Andrew Wawn, Keneva Kunz, Terry Gunnell, Ruth C. Ellison, Martin S. Regal, Katrina C. Attwood, George Clark, and Anthony Maxwell, trans. *Sagas of the Icelanders*. With a preface by Jane Smiley and an introduction by Robert Kellogg. New York, Viking Press, 1997.

Sheffield, Ann Gróa. *Frey, God of the World:* Meadville, Pa., published by Medoburg Kindred, 2003.

Simek, Rudolf. *Dictionary of Northern Mythology*. Cambridge, England: D.S. Brewer, 1993.

Strmiska, Michael. "Ásatrú in Iceland: the Rebirth of Nordic Paganism?" *Nova Religio* 4.1 (2000): 106–132.

———. "The Evils of Christianization: A Pagan Perspective on European History." Conference on Perspectives on Evil and Human Wickedness, Prague, Czech Republic, March 2002.

Sturluson, Snorri. *The Heimskringla*. Translated by A.H. Smith. New York: Dover Publications, 1990.

———. *The Poetic Edda*. Translated by Carolyne Larrington. Oxford, England: Oxford University Press, 1996.

———. *The Poetic Edda*. Translated by Henry Bellows. London: Oxford University Press, 1926.

———. *The Poetic Edda*. Translated by Lee Hollander. Austin, Tex.: University of Texas Press, 1994.

———. *The Poetic Edda*. Translated by W.H. Auden and Paul Taylor. London: Faber and Faber, 1969.

———. *The Prose Edda.* Translated by Jean Young. Berkely, Calif.: University of California Press, 1954.

Tacitus, Cornelius. *Germania*. Translated by J. B. Rives. Oxford: Clarendon Press, 1999.

Thorsson, Edred. *Futhark*. York Beach, Maine: Samuel Weiser, 1984.

———. *Runelore*. York Beach, Maine: Samuel Weiser, 1987.

Turville-Petre, Gabriel. *Myth and Religion in the North: The Religion of Ancient Scandinavia*. London: Weidenfeld & Nicholson, 1964.

Tzu, Sun. *The Art of War*. Translated by Thomas Cleary. Boston: Shambhala Publications, 1988.

Wallis, Robert. *Shamans/Neo-Shamans: Ecstasy, Alternative Archaeologies and Contemporary Pagans*. New York: Routledge, 2003.

Ward, Christy. "Women and Magic in the Sagas." Located in "Art" menu, http://www.vikinganswerlady.com (accessed April 2, 2003).

Wodening, Eric. "Knowest How to Blót." http://wodening.ealdriht.org/eric/blot.html (accessed October 9, 2004).

———. *The Rites of Heathendom*. San Leandro, Calif.: Café Press, 2003.

———. The Threefold Initiation of Woden. New York: Theod, n.d.

———. *We Are Our Deeds:* New York, Theod Press, 1998.

Wodening, Swain. "Anglo-Saxon Witchcraft." *Marklander* 66 (2003): 9–11.

———. *Hammer of the Gods*. Little Elm: Imprint Books, 2003.

———. "Holda and the Cult of the Witches." *Marklander* 64 (2002): 2–7.

———. *The Witegungseld Spá and Oracular Seiðr Manual*. N.p.: published by Angel Seaxisce Ealdriht, 2003.

Suggested Reading

Heathens pride themselves on being well read both about their faith and the historical period in which it originally evolved. Many even go so far as to study the ancient languages: Old Norse, Old English, and Gothic, as well as modern Icelandic and German. Studying the lore is one of the primary devotional practices in modern Heathenry and even minute points of controversy are discussed avidly. Following is a basic list of suggested resources to help the newcomer become fairly well versed in Heathen lore. This is *far* from a complete list, but the books named are essential and will provide a thorough foundation from which the reader may branch out.

- ***The Poetic Edda* by Snorri Sturluson**

  This is the "holy" book of modern Heathens. There are numerous translations available and it is generally advisable to read at least three or four different versions. The most commonly available are those translated by Carolyn Larrington (Oxford University Press) and Lee Hollander (Texas University Press). Older translations by Henry Bellows (American Scandinavian Foundation) and Olive Bray (AMS Press) are generally considered preferable, but they are more difficult to find as the volumes are out of print. Online specialty bookshops, such as *www.abebooks.com* and *www.amazon.com*, are a godsend for Heathens, and it is possible to find out-of-print books at a fairly reasonable price.

- ***The Prose Edda* by Snorri Sturluson**

  This is a prose retelling of the tales found in the Poetic Edda and is also a "must read." The two most popular versions are by Jean Young (University of California Press) and Anthony Faulkes (The Everyman Library). American Scandinavian Society published a translation by Arthur Brodeur, which is considered one of the superior translations.

- ***Norse Myths* by Kevin Crossley-Holland (Pantheon Books, 1980)**

  Norse Myths is an entertaining retelling of the Eddic tales, and it is rather like CliffsNotes to the Eddas. It's an excellent and very approachable book that should grace the shelves of any beginner's library.

- ***Hammer of the Gods* by Swain Wodening (Imprint Books, 2003)**

  This is the first introductory book published that deals exclusively with Anglo-Saxon Heathenry. The author is the cofounder of Thæt Angelseaxisce Ealdriht and an elder within modern Heathenry. It is an excellent introduction to modern practice and theology and an invaluable resource to newcomers. This book discusses cosmology, ethics, lore, holidays, and rituals within the Anglo-Saxon denomination. It is a seminal work in its field.

- ***Teutonic Religion* by Kveldulf Gundarsson (Llewellyn, 1993)**

  This was one of the very first books written on modern Heathenry and was very influential within Asatru. The author is an elder within the Troth and contributed widely to the source material available on their Website (*www.thetroth.org*). The book is a solid reference that discusses every aspect of Heathen practice and custom.

- ***Gods and Myths of Northern Europe*** **by H.R. Ellis Davidson (Penguin Books, 1990)**

  This is one of the first books generally recommended to newcomers. It is a scholarly work discussing the Norse Gods and the culture in which They were originally worshipped. It's an invaluable companion to the Eddas, and the reader will come away with a firm understanding of each of the Gods, though it should be kept in mind that the author is not a practicing Heathen.

- ***The Road to Hel*** **by H.R. Ellis Davidson (Greenwood Press, 1968)**

  The Road to Hel discusses the concept of death and the afterlife in Heathen Cosmology. Funeral customs, the soul parts, and the various possible destinations in the afterlife are covered in detail. This is the seminal work on the topic and, along with the following book listed, invaluable. Sadly, it is out of print and very difficult to find, but it's worth scouring libraries and asking among local Heathens for copies.

- ***The Well and the Tree*** **by Paul Bauschatz (The University of Massachusetts, 1982)**

  Bauschatz examines the concept of wyrd within Heathen Cosmological thought. He examines the role of Urtha's Well, Yggdrasil, and the idea of layering fate. This is an exceptional book and, as far as I know, the only scholarly work on the subject. Sadly, it is out of print, but worth the trouble of tracking down. Like *Road to Hel*, this book is invaluable to a thorough understanding of wyrd, orlog, and fate, within Heathenry. Modern Heathens owe this scholar a great debt for this work alone.

- ***Beowulf***

  A great deal of knowledge about Anglo-Saxon holy customs can be gleaned from *Beowulf*. There are numerous translations available. Of particular interest are the dual text versions by Seamus Heaney (W.W. Norton & Company, 2000) and Howell Chickering, Jr. (Anchor Books, 1977).

- ***Dictionary of Northern Mythology* by Rudolf Simek (D.S. Brewer, 2000)**

  This is a wonderful compendium for any Heathen or scholar. Simek has compiled an exhaustive dictionary of Heathen terms encompassing heroes, Gods, names, and concepts found throughout the lore. This book is an invaluable reference and the most thorough currently available. It covers the entire history of Germanic culture and religion, and I would suggest making it one's first purchase after the Eddas.

- ***Rites and Religions of the Anglo-Saxons* by Gale Owen (Barnes & Noble Books, 1981)**

  This book examines Anglo-Saxon pre-Christian religion and culture. Though very basic, it is useful for developing an understanding of the historical roots of modern Anglo-Saxon Heathenry.

- ***The Lost Gods of England* by Brian Branston (Oxford University Press, 1974)**

  A fascinating volume that examines surviving Christian texts for clues to Anglo-Saxon Heathen worship, Branston has given us a valuable resource for modern Anglo-Saxon Heathens. Because England converted earlier than any other Germanic country, much of its cosmology and lore was lost. Branston attempts a valuable reconstruction from the surviving fragments and does much to enhance our understanding of the English Gods.

- ***Gods of the North* by Brian Branston (Thames & Hudson Press, 1980)**

  Branston examines Eddic cosmology and discusses each of the main Gods and Goddesses in turn, examining the folklore and beliefs surrounding Them. It's a valuable resource—equal, in my opinion, to H.R. Ellis Davidson's *Gods and Myths of Northern Europe*.

- ***The Sagas of the Icelanders* edited by Örnólfr Thorsson (Viking Press, 2000)**

  This is a collection of several influential Icelandic Sagas including *Egil's Saga*. While entertaining stories in their own rite, modern Heathens look to these sagas for clues to pre-Christian religious practices. Additionally, one should read the following sagas listed.

- ***Eyrbyggja Saga*** **translated by Hermann Pálsson (Penguin Books, 1989)**

  A saga replete with magic, treachery, cunning, and political maneuvering, *Eyrbyggja Saga* provides a unique glimpse into the social structure, political climate, and surviving folk practices in Iceland shortly after its conversion.

- ***Njal's Saga*** **translated by Robert Cook (Penguin Books, 2001)**

  One of the most famous sagas, this tale of murder and blood feud chronicles the era of transition from Heathenry to Christianity in Iceland.

- ***The Anglo-Saxon World: An Anthology*** **translated by Kevin Crossley-Holland (Oxford University Press, 1982)**

  This book is a compendium of the major Anglo-Saxon texts. Though the majority of them are overtly Christian, they provide many clues to folk practices and Heathen cultural mores and are valuable resources for that purpose.

- ***Myth and Religion of the North*** **by E.O.G. Turville-Petre (Greenwood Press, 1964)**

  This book examines the religion, Gods, and culture of pre-Christian Northern Europe, offering an examination of the lore, beliefs, and practices of the Arch-Heathens that dramatically increases understanding of the nature of the Gods. It stands with *Road to Hel* and *The Well and the Tree* as an essential volume for thorough understanding of Heathen lore.

- ***The Whisperings of Woden*** **by Galina Krasskova (Global Book Publishers, 2004)**

  This was the first Heathen devotional to be published specifically for the God Woden. It offers meditations and devotional prayers to help the votary develop a relationship with this God. The prayers and exercises given may be adapted for any God or Goddess and provide a more personal means of honoring the Gods than usually presented in lore-based sources.

- ***We Are Our Deeds* Eric Wodening (Theod Press, 1998)**

  This slender volume examines Heathen ethics, thew, and the concept of good and evil within Heathenry, both ancient and modern. While not necessarily "easy" reading, it is essential to any understanding of modern Heathen values.

Once the preceding books have been acquired and studied, further advanced resources may be found in the bibliography.

Index

C

D

E

F

G

About the Author

Originally ordained in 1995 in the Fellowship of Isis, Reverend Galina Krasskova converted to Heathenry in 1996, after several potent experiences with Odin. For many years she was acting Priestess-Hierophant of a Fellowship of Isis Lyceum in New York and credits the Fellowship of Isis with paving the way for her conversion to Heathenry. In 2000, Galina graduated from and was ordained by The New Seminary, an interfaith seminary in New York, where she is now registered with that state as a minister. From 1999 until 2001, Galina was on the faculty at the seminary as lecturer in Pagan religions. She currently serves as a mentor to first-year students within the seminary and is also editor of the "featured religion" section of The New Seminary's Newsletter.

Galina is weofodthignen (priest) of Urdabrunnr Kindred (*urda.seika.org*) in New York City, Blotestere (ritual priest) within Néoweanglia Maethel, and has been an active member of the Heathen community since 1996. Galina is cofounder of the New York Metro Asatru Society, which holds public rites and seminars several times a year in an effort to better educate the Pagan community about Heathenry. Additionally, as a priest, she maintains an active pastoral counseling practice.

Galina lectures and teaches within the New York Pagan and Heathen communities on Heathen-related issues. She is a frequent contributor to such respected Pagan and Heathen magazines as *Sagewoman*, *NewWitch*, *Idunna*, *The Ealdriht Bóc*, and *Marklander*. In addition to *Exploring the Northern Tradition*, Galina has published a book of Woden devotionals titled *The Whisperings of Woden*. In her spare time, Galina studies the martial arts—particularly Iaido and Kendo—and the Icelandic language. She may be reached at tamyris@nerdalfheim.org.